I0016857

Lindemann Group

Peter Schiessl

Microsoft

PowerPoint 2024

EXCEPTIONALLY SIMPLE

TRAINING BOOK WITH MANY EXERCISES

ISBN 979-8-314791-94-3
Print on Demand since June, 28th 2023
Translated into English (US) by Peter Schiessl
V250320 / LINDEMANN Group
Publisher: Lindemann BHIT, Munich
Postal address: LE/Schiessl, Fortnerstr. 8, 80933 Munich, Germany
E-Mail: post@kamiprint.de / Telefax: 0049 (0)89 99 95 46 83
© MSc. (UAS) Peter Schiessl, Munich, Germany
www.lindemann-beer.com / www.kamiprint.de

This book was created end of 2024 from a complete installation of MS Office 2024 on Windows 11. Deviations from the descriptions and illustrations are possible due to a user-defined installation or changes due to other installed software or updates.

Table of Contents

SUPPLEMENTARY_____ 125

Chapter

1

1. WHAT IS POWERPOINT?

PowerPoint is a program that you can use to create presentations.

- ◆ This is comparable to a presentation with a slide projector.
  - ↳ With the slide projector, you can show different slides one after the other.
  - ↳ With PowerPoint, these slides (=slides) are combined in a presentation, similar to a folder for slides. You can scroll to the next slide with a mouse click or let the presentation run automatically.

- ◆ You can show these presentations on the screen,
  - ↳ e.g., when you present your product to customers,
  - ↳ or let it run automatically, e.g., on a computer in the shop window of your shop.

- ◆ You can print out the presentations on overhead transparencies and present them in the classic way at meetings, customer visits, trade fairs or as a lecturer using an overhead projector.
  - ↳ Special films that you can print with any inkjet or laser printer
  - ↳ are available at any computer store or from the office suppliers.

PowerPoint offers numerous aids and effects to make these slides effective and appealing:

- ◆ Wizards make it easier to create slides.
  - ↳ You can choose between suggestions, e.g., invitation or works meeting and only have to overwrite the texts.

- ◆ A beautiful graphical background creates a professional look in no time.

- ◆ Special animations, e.g., the typewriter effect with the corresponding sound, increase attention and make the presentation more varied.

Text with multiple columns:

- ♦ PowerPoint is not ideal for multi-column layouts.
  - ↳ Multiple columns can be created in any text program.
  - ↳ PowerPoint is designed for consecutive slides with little text, a nice background and animations.
  - ↳ Multiple columns can only be reached in PowerPoint by placing multiple text frames next to each other.

Note if you use inkjet printers:

- ♦ Inkjet printouts are usually not waterproof.
  - ↳ There is a risk that these will smear during transport or on the projector.
  - ↳ To prevent this, you can insert the slides in transparent sleeves. Special foils for overhead projectors are recommended.
  - ↳ These are wafer-thin so that the foil does not have to be removed for the presentation and have suitable perforations for projectors.
- ♦ As an alternative, the films can be sealed with a special clear coat. However, painting requires manual skill.

Notes: ....

....

....

....

....

....

....

....

....

....

....

....

....

Chapter 2

2. ABOUT THE DESIGN

With PowerPoint, you can create beautifully designed presentations relatively easily. We don't want to bore you with all the possible rules of advertising, market and perception psychology, but only give you a few design tips, since PowerPoint does most of the work using templates and ready-made designs.

2.1 ISSUE

The end product is what matters. The main difference here is whether you want to show your presentation on the screen or print it out.

About the quality:

- For the screen presentation, the resolution on the output monitor should be based on what is usual today: Full HD 1920x1080 pixels or even 4k: 3,840x2,160.

- In the case of a printout, the output medium determines the quality, mostly 300 dpi (dots per inch) on transparencies, and up to 9600 dpi in offset printing.

For font size:

These quality specifications are to be taken into account above all with the font size, since with poor screen or television resolution only large fonts with at least 12 pt. may be used, while with perfect print media small fonts with 9 points or even 8 points can be used for longer information texts.

- In the case of display on the monitor, numerous slides are therefore necessary, each with only a small amount of very large text. In the case of printed information, if longer texts are required, pages with compressed facts in small fonts can also be distributed.

- However, the important information should always be presented briefly and precisely on separate slides.

For color choice:

With printed output, everything is possible with perfect print quality (color laser or offset printing), but there are narrow limits on conventional inkjet printers, since the colors often run and dark backgrounds in particular are problematic.

- ♦ A trick: black font runs the most, so use dark tones for the text instead of black font.

- ♦ All printers are different, display colors slightly differently, have problems with some colors: make test prints early.

- ♦ With inkjet printers, optimal output is only possible on transparencies or coated glossy paper.
  - ♥ With inkjet printers, the quality setting is important for optimal printouts; the correct type of paper and the desired quality must be specified (File/Print, then select "Properties" for the printer).

2.2 PRELIMINARY DESIGN CONSIDERATIONS

When designing, the first consideration is the output medium, the second is which customers the project is intended for. For your presentation to be well received, it must be adapted to the customer's taste. This is best illustrated with examples.

- ♦ In the case of a private birthday invitation for children, the design cannot be colorful enough and it is best to set each letter in a different font size, type and color, the same applies to a website for young people.

- ♦ A more serious, aesthetic design is preferable for a company presentation or almost any other application. Too many colors, too many different fonts or other special effects should be avoided.
  - ♥ Note professional advertisements. Typically, a base color is used that matches the product, such as coffee gold, brown, or royal blue, but not yellow or purple.
  - ♥ Many companies use a basic color and uniform company logos to achieve the impression of "corporate identity".

- ♦ Colors from standardized color palettes, e.g., Pantone, are used so that such colors always look the same, regardless of whether they are printed on business cards, stationery or advertising flyers.
  - ♥ Every print shop has catalogues in which these standardized colors are printed so that the color can be mixed together identically.

- ♦ When it comes to the font, only one font should be used for the text, and if necessary, a stronger font for the headings.
  - ♥ Use stronger fonts for the screen presentation, these are easier to read on the screen or in slide presentations.

FIRST PRESENTATIONS

Start and save a presentation, enter text, select view

3. THE POWERPOINT STRUCTURE

➤ Start this with Start/PowerPoint (Start = the Windows icon at the bottom). You can now

Open

↳ on the left open a presentation you have already created with "Open" or

↳ start a new "empty presentation"

More themes →

↳ or start with a template, additional templates are displayed if you click "More themes", in the window that appears you can enter a search term, e.g., "flowers", to find a matching preset.

New

➤ Start a new presentation with a template by clicking on a template, confirm with "Create". That was quick and easy!

Now we can take a closer look at the PowerPoint structure.

3.1 THE SYMBOLS IN THE RIBBON

The commands are sorted into corresponding index cards, e.g. an overview can be found under Home or under Insert various elements such as photos, shapes, text fields, etc. can be inserted.

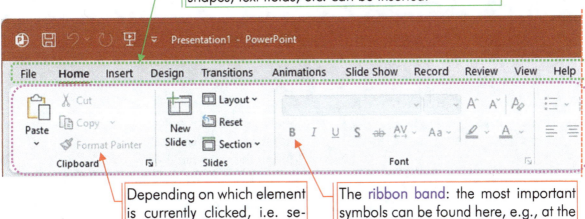

Depending on which element is currently clicked, i.e. selected, options are available or disabled.

The ribbon band: the most important symbols can be found here, e.g., at the start, B to make selected text bold.

The Working Area:

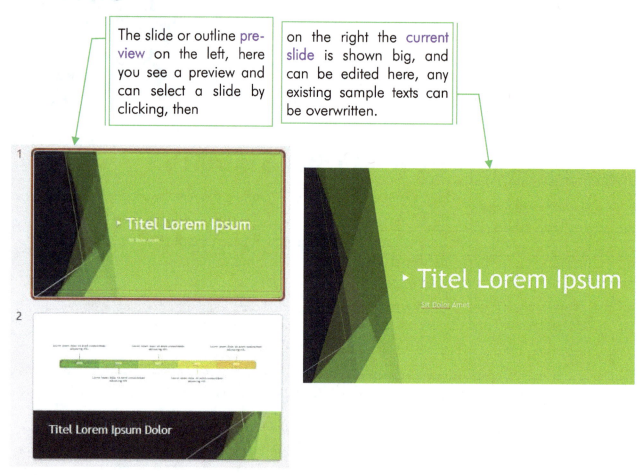

The slide or outline pre-view on the left, here you see a preview and can select a slide by clicking, then

on the right the current slide is shown big, and can be edited here, any existing sample texts can be overwritten.

3.2 THE STATUS BAR AND ZOOM

At the bottom of the window, you will find the status bar:

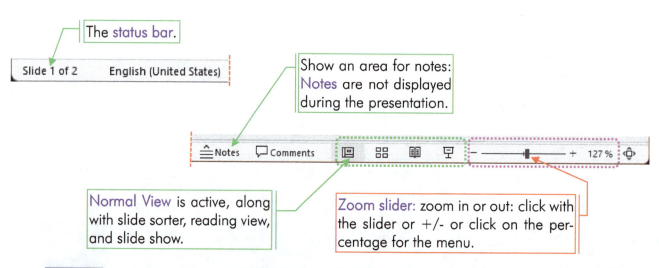

The status bar.

Slide 1 of 2   English (United States)

Show an area for notes: Notes are not displayed during the presentation.

Normal View is active, along with slide sorter, reading view, and slide show.

Zoom slider: zoom in or out: click with the slider or +/- or click on the percentage for the menu.

3.3 IMPORTANT ELEMENTS OF POWERPOINT

◆ The PowerPoint bar is at the top. The name of the current presentation is displayed next to Microsoft PowerPoint.

    ✎ If it says Presentation 1 (2, 3 …) – PowerPoint, the presentation has never been saved! Save as soon as possible!

◆ Then follows the menu bar with the commands.

    ✎ Press e.g., on Insert. There you can insert images, photos, comments, text fields, headers and much more.

    ✎ Go through the other tabs: File - Start...

◆ Below that, the ribbon bar for frequently used commands.

    ✎ Symbols are abbreviations for frequently used commands.

    ✎ Depending on the size of the PowerPoint window and the resolution of your screen, only symbols or symbols with labels are displayed, so the display varies depending on the window size.

3.4 TO ALL COMMANDS

Not all icons have space, so only the most important ones are shown. You can get to the complete menu with all commands as follows, here using the example of the font settings at start:

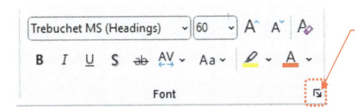

If available, click on this small expansion arrow and the complete command menu with all setting options will open. Note that some menus have multiple tabs.

This is the case for all symbol groups, if there is no expansion arrow there are no further commands in this group.

Complete the exercise:

➢ Scroll through the slides, use Home/Replace to replace the year with the current year, of course the days would also have to be adjusted to the current year.

2nd Section

TEXT AND TEXT BOX

Enter and format text, slide layout and design, set, move, delete text fields

4. TEXT AND TEXT BOX

Now the presentation is adjusted. We will overwrite text, add or delete pages, and try different display styles.

➢ Close (File/Close) the slides you opened as a test without saving and select a template again, e.g., Madison or ION Boardroom.

> Text is entered in text fields. Usually there are already two text frames; if you click on them, they become visible in the selection frames.:

♦ We can use the existing text frames, move them and adjust their size as needed, or draw new text frames using Insert/Text Box like a rectangle in the slide with the mouse button pressed.

4.1 SET TEXT BOX

As soon as you click on the text in the preview area, the frame will be visible and the frame of the frame appears. It applies:

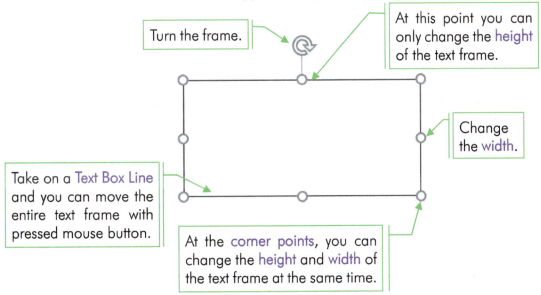

As a result, the text can be easily and arbitrarily moved to this frame.

➢ Enter the text as shown in the text frames, at the end of the line, if necessary, start a new paragraph with Return.

↳ If you have chosen a template without two text fields, use Insert/Text Field to insert new text frames if necessary. Unnecessary text frames can be clicked and deleted with [Del].

➢ Format as shown, e.g., by marking the heading and then setting a suitable font, color and size at the start.

➢ Finally, arrange both text frames accordingly.

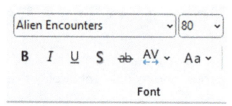

You can use existing text frames and resize them or create new ones: Insert/Text Box, then draw them like a rectangle.

4.2 TIPS FOR MARKING

The computer needs to know which word or phrase we want to change. Therefore, the text passage to be changed must first be marked. Only then can the font setting be varied.

◆ A word by double-clicking with the mouse.

◆ A whole paragraph by three quick clicks.

To mark

◆ Longer sections with the [Shift] key pressed, then the [Direction] or [pg up] / [pg dn] key.

↳ Only release the [Shift] key as soon as the marking fits!

↳ You can select the [Direction] or [pg up] / [pg dn] button in the other direction to reduce the marking.

◆ Longer sections with the mouse: hold down the left mouse button and drag over the point to be marked.

4.3 NEW LINE OR NEW PARAGRAPH

Note the important difference:

- ♦ With [Return] you start a new paragraph.
  - ↳ The settings are adopted from the previous paragraph, e.g., the bullet point or the font settings of the heading.

- ♦ Use [Shift]-[Return] to start a new line in the same paragraph so that the paragraph settings are not changed.

4.4 ADD PAGE

Now that we have a nice, clear presentation, we can practice adding a new page (=slide).

> Trick: copy the text frames, then you can paste it on the new slides and just overwrite the text, so the identical font and paragraph settings are adopted.

- ➢ Mark the whole text frame, copy, new slide with:
  - ↳ Home/New Slide
  - ↳ or Insert/New Slide
  - ↳ or the keyboard shortcut [Ctrl]–M

  [Ctrl]–M
  - ↳ or right-click/New Slide in the outline area on the left- click in the empty area, not on an existing slide.

- ➢ On the new slide you can now paste the previously copied text frame, so we have adopted all the font settings and only need to overwrite the text as desired.

- ➢ Add more slides, copy the text frames there and overwrite them, e.g., as follows:

After the font has been formatted as desired, adjust the text frames and arrange them correctly.

Suggestions for the further slides:

GRADUATION CELEBRATION

- **Sunday 1st August**
- **From 3pm**
- **At Shirley Chisholm State Park**

Address
Fountain Side
950 Fountain Avenue
Brooklyn, NY 11239

Spacing

Before: 6 pt

After: 6 pt

Set the font and paragraphs appropriately, e.g., with a favourable paragraph spacing before and after the paragraphs (right mouse button/paragraph).

Please bring:

- **Something to grill**
- **Or salads**
- **Or chips and candy**
- **Or drinks**

Bullet points you will find at home/paragraph:

Registration and Questions:

- **Phone: 123 123 123 123**
- **Telefax: 123 123 123 124**
- **E-Mail: mymail@mymail.uk**
- **Or Alphorn: Trooo Tuuu TroTro**

If your mouse has a wheel, when the cursor is in the preview area, you can use the mouse wheel to scroll through each slide.

4.5 FOIL LAYOUT

Afterwards you can still beautify the foils, these three possible possibilities are particularly recommended:

- In the case of Home/Quick Styles, a new quick format template (= colored frame filling and font formatting) can be selected for a marked frame.

- Another page layout can be selected at the Home/Layout.

- A different foil design or other color composition can be selected in the command bar by Design.

➢ Try by some slides a Quick Style and different Layouts and Designs:

Notes: ....

....

....

....

....

....

....

....

....

....

....

Chapter

5

5. SAVE PRESENTATION

We want to save the new presentation immediately. On the one hand, the question arises where we save, on the other hand, this is a good opportunity to present the different alternatives, to perform actions.

5.1 CREATE A FOLDER

There are numerous ways to carry out certain functions (commands). The following standards are common:

- All commands are sorted in the Command Bar under suitable key-words: File / Home / Insert etc.
    - ✍ Here you can click on a menu item with the mouse, e.g., at File you will find both Save and Save Under
    - ✍ or with a keyboard shortcut if defined, e.g., [Ctrl] -S for saving.

You can also find saving here as a symbol at the top left, this should be a floppy disk, which is no longer known today.

We want to store all of our exercise presentations in our own folder so that we can easily find them and secure them regularly at any time. We can create this folder when saving the first exercise.

- ➤ Choose Save, then "More options…" and "Browse", the folders of your drives are displayed.

- ➤ Click the "Documents" folder, then we can create a new folder here.

Create a new folder with this icon.

- ➤ The new folder is already open for renaming, so you can write the name "Exercises PowerPoint 2024" directly and complete with Return.
    - ✍ If this worked, the newly created folder can still be opened with a double-click or return.

♦ If the naming did not work, right-click on the new folder and "Re-name", then return twice again to confirm and open,

↳ in Windows 11, first select "Show more options" to open the complete drop-down menu including the "Rename" command.

➢ Now the file name for the presentation has to be entered, PowerPoint suggests the title here, which we can keep:

After "Save" the presentation is saved as a file with the name "Computer Driving License" in the newly created folder.

| File name: | Computer Driving License |
| Save as type: | PowerPoint Presentation (*.pptx) |

5.2 OPENING FILES

♦ Immediately after starting PowerPoint and in the File menu, the most recently edited files are displayed.

↳ Here you can expand the selection with "More presentations" or use "Browse" to display and open other presentations from your hard disk or other drives, such as USB sticks.

More presentations →

↳ Especially if you save your work in a separate folder on your hard disk, it is also a good idea to open the desired presentation from Windows Explorer by double-clicking it.

➢ Close the presentation with File/Close and open it again.

5.3 EXIT POWERPOINT, CHANGE WINDOW SIZE

➢ Start another presentation with a template. This is opened in a separate window.

➢ With [Alt]-[Tab] you can switch between the windows. Hold down [Alt] and use [Tab] to select the desired window.

↳ You can also change the active window at the bottom of the start bar by clicking on the entry for the desired window.

➢ You will find these symbols at the top right:

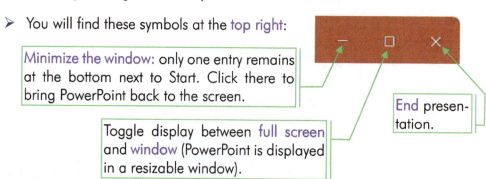

Minimize the window: only one entry remains at the bottom next to Start. Click there to bring PowerPoint back to the screen.

Toggle display between full screen and window (PowerPoint is displayed in a resizable window).

End presentation.

6. SET VIEW

In each view, it is practical to set the size of the display to be in a matching manner: For work on the text, as much as possible, in order not to overlook any errors, a reduced view before printing to check the entire page on the screen.

With View/Zoom you can open the zoom menu:

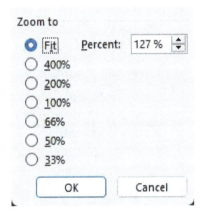

- ◆ You can change the area limits, for example, between the thumbnail (left) and foil (right) area with the mouse:

  ☝ Move the mouse across the area limit, when the mouse arrow changes to double arrow, move with the mouse button pressed.

- ◆ The above zoom buttons always apply to the currently active area.

  ☝ This also allows you to adjust the size of the slide preview on the left by clicking there first.

- ◆ In both areas, you can use "Fit" to optimally adjust the size to the window size.

> Practical: if you have a wheel mouse, you can also enlarge or reduce the view with the mouse wheel when the [Ctrl] key is pressed.

The button at the bottom right of the start bar is faster:

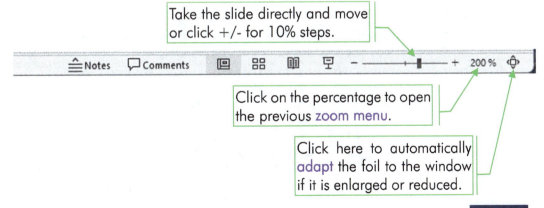

Take the slide directly and move or click +/- for 10% steps.

Click on the percentage to open the previous zoom menu.

Click here to automatically adapt the foil to the window if it is enlarged or reduced.

6.1 CHANGE THE VIEW

♦ So far, we have worked in the "Normal" view:

    ↳ left the outline view with overview slides and

    ↳ the preview window on the right, in which we can see the finished foils.

At the bottom right you will find these symbols with which you can change the display type. Corresponding commands are housed in View.

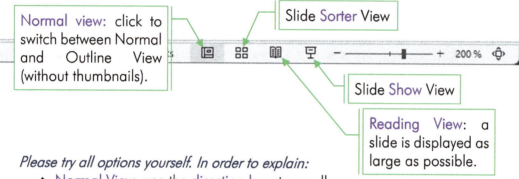

Normal view: click to switch between Normal and Outline View (without thumbnails).

Slide Sorter View

Slide Show View

Reading View: a slide is displayed as large as possible.

Please try all options yourself. In order to explain:

♦ Normal View: use the direction keys to scroll.

♦ You see all slides reduced in the Slide Sorter View.

    ↳ Again, on the icon or icon Normal View or by double-clicking on a slide you get back to the normal view, whereby this slide is then selected.

    ↳ In this view, you can drag a slide to a different position to change the order.

[Esc]   ♦ Reading View: the largest possible display of the current slide, the easiest way is to return to the Normal View with [Esc].

♦ With the Slide Show, the presentation runs like on a slide projector, only on the screen.

    ↳ You can scroll forwards or backwards with a mouse click, the [Page Up/Page Down] keys or the Direction Keys [Up/Down].

    ↳ With [Esc] you can cancel a presentation.

6.2 UNDO

Adjusting text and background is only possible with a lot of trial and error. That's why the Undo Icon is very useful.

♦ Almost nothing can happen to you with the following advice:
    ↳ Observe the result on the screen for each action. If what is expected does not happen, select Undo immediately.
    ↳ Find out the cause (wrong command, not marked, etc.) and look for the right command.

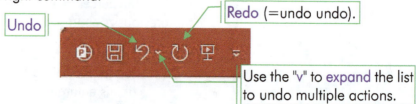

Redo (=undo undo).

Undo

Use the "v" to expand the list to undo multiple actions.

7. FORMAT TEXT

7.1 NEW PRESENTATION

We create a new presentation.

➢ Close the previous exercise and select File/New again and start a new presentation using one of the numerous PowerPoint templates.

✍ These templates are simply too beautiful and numerous to create another presentation from scratch.

✍ Since we want to present a solar house, a template with a yellow or sun reference is recommended; the "Facet" template was used below. If you can't find this template in the thumbnails, just search for facet in "Search for …".

✍ However, you can also select a different template and adjust the colors accordingly later.

7.2 CUSTOMIZE TEXT

➢ Overwrite the text with this sample text, preferably in two text fields, one for the solar house and one for the address.

➢ Try different designs on the Design tab and different fillings for the text boxes by "Shape Format/Shape Fill" or "Shape Designs".

New Slide ⌄

➢ Now to the next foil, right mouse button on the left in the outline view and "New Slide" or the symbol at Home:

2 ▢ **Project Goals**
   ◆ Supporting power generation by solar systems,
   ◆ minimal energy consumption through optimal thermal insulation,
   ◆ healthy living climate through breathable bricks,
   ◆ pleasant atmosphere due to extensive outdoor vegetation,
   ◆ low additional construction costs due to standard elements,
   ◆ low maintenance costs due to solid construction.

➢ And now a third slide:

The Sponsors of the Project

The project is supported and supported by

- Solar-Sun Example Ltd.,
- the Faculty of Architecture of the University of Sampling City and
- the Institute for Building Materials Science in Everywhere City.

For more convenient formatting, a practical tool will be presented in the next chapter.

7.3 SET FONT

The presentation is again largely preset.

➢ Look at the presentation in the different views and let the presentation run on the screen.

You will find the most important setting options for text in the ribbon toolbar by Home. The text is arranged in frames. Note that you must either select text or click the frame before you can change the settings.

The font settings at Home:

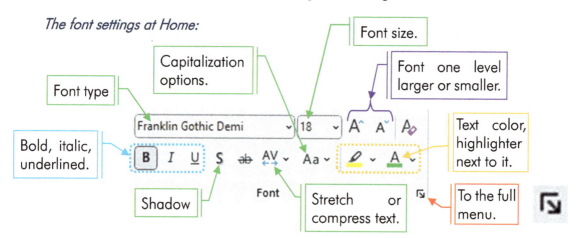

The full menu could also be opened with the right mouse button/Font (click right mouse button over the already highlighted text to be set).

For example, you can use superscript for times such as:

$$\text{"Saturday at } 7^{30} \text{ p.m."}$$

➢ Highlight the heading and set a yellow shadow for the text box with Right Mouse Button/Format Text Effects:

↳ First choose a preset, then the color for the shadow.

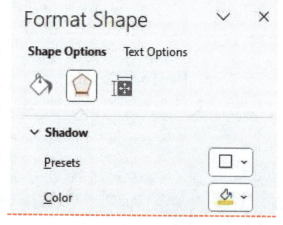

7.4 MODIFY TEXT BOX

When you click a text, the Text Box appears. You can change the size of this text frame using the handles or grab and move it along a line.

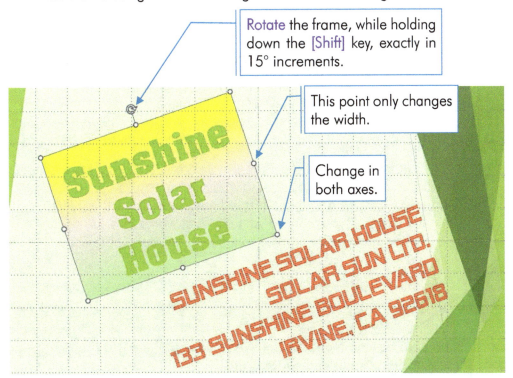

Rotate the frame, while holding down the [Shift] key, exactly in 15° increments.

This point only changes the width.

Change in both axes.

➤ Right mouse button on the frame, then set a gradient fill in "Format Shape", likewise right mouse button on the background and in "Format Background". Or at Design/Format Background.

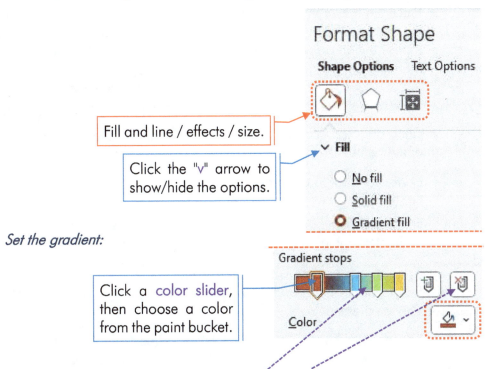

Fill and line / effects / size.

Click the "v" arrow to show/hide the options.

Set the gradient:

Click a color slider, then choose a color from the paint bucket.

♦ Double-click to set new color sliders, delete: drag a slider out of the bar with the left mouse button pressed or use the symbol on the right.

If you want to format and arrange a piece of text differently, it's a good idea to create another frame, since text in its own frame can be dragged to any desired position with the mouse.

♦ With the Insert/Text Box command, you can open another text frame on the slide while holding down the mouse button, then start writing immediately so that the text is entered.

♦ If you want to split a frame, mark the part of the text that should be in the new frame, then cut it out with [Ctrl]-x, open a new frame with Insert/Text Box and insert the text with [Ctrl]-v there.

[Ctrl]-c = copy,
[Ctrl]-x = cut out,
[Ctrl]-v = insert.

> See picture in next chapter format painter.

If you select a frame and make text settings, these apply to all text within the frame. If you want to set individual words in a targeted manner, they must first be marked with the mouse button pressed.

7.5 FORMAT PAINTER

So that you don't have to mark and set every heading, there is a practical tool: Format Painter to transfer the formatting.

➢ Format the heading "Project Goals" particularly large.
  ↳ Large font (66pt), bold font (e.g., Arial Black) with a different color and shadow and underlined.

➢ Place the cursor in the heading that has just been set, then click on "Format Painter" at Home and mark the next heading, e.g., with the mouse button pressed or by clicking to the left of the heading in the margin.

How it works:

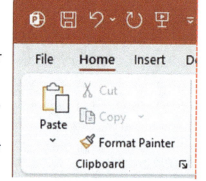

♦ Click once on "Format Painter" for one-time use

♦ or double-click to perform this function multiple times.
  ↳ To switch off, click on "Format Painter" again.

The Format Painter method works just as well for single words. Then mark the words to be formatted with a double click or several words with the mouse button pressed.

➢ Add another page, e.g., "Schedule" or "Already implemented" with suitable text and format it identically to the previous slides.

➢ Finally, save the project in our exercise folder.

Chapter 8

8. PARAGRAPH SETTINGS

8.1 BULLET SWITCH

➤ Add this text to another final slide:

> **Inquiries to:**
> ◆ **Dr. Walter Smith**
>   **Phone: 67 67 67 67 67**
> ◆ **Prof. Dr. Matt Million**
>   **Phone: 191919191**

First a new line with [Ctrl]-[Return], then a new paragraph with [Return], since a bullet point is placed in front of each paragraph.

You can easily add the bullet point with the symbol shown on the left after you have selected the two paragraphs of text. A different bullet point would be nicer though.

➤ Mark both paragraphs, press the right mouse button on them and at Bullets in the drop-down menu (click the arrow) continue to "Bullets and Numbering":

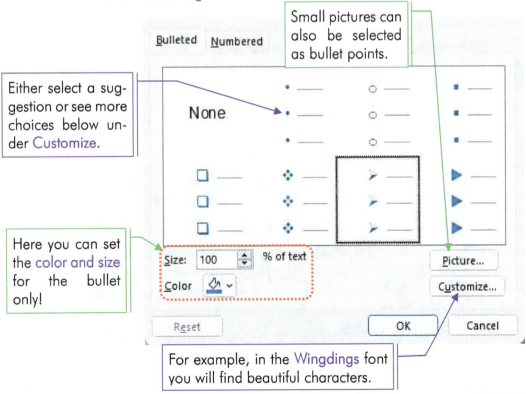

Small pictures can also be selected as bullet points.

Either select a suggestion or see more choices below under Customize.

Here you can set the color and size for the bullet only!

For example, in the Wingdings font you will find beautiful characters.

8.1.1 SET BULLETS

A lot can be done with the two buttons Picture and Customize.

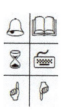

♦ Under Customize you can choose other font symbols, of which there are very nice ones, e.g., in the fonts Wingdings and Webdings.

    ↳ Such fonts only contain small images instead of letters.

    ↳ Many programs contain other such special fonts, so you should browse through the fonts installed on your computer and get an overview.

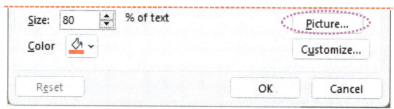

♦ The Picture button allows you to use small, colored images as bullet points, with the following options:

    ↳ "From a File" = find and use photos from your computer,

    ↳ "Stock Images": a PowerPoint collection of photos and pictograms that offers a wide range of choices,

    ↳ "Online Pictures" = photo galleries from the Internet with the Microsoft search engine Bing or

    ↳ "From Icons" = symbol images included with PowerPoint can be used as bullet points.

„Stock Images" and "From Icons" opens the same menu, except that the Images tab is selected instead of icons tab, in which some interesting options are well hidden:

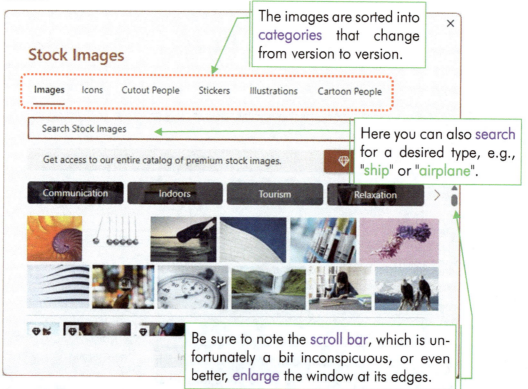

The images are sorted into categories that change from version to version.

Here you can also search for a desired type, e.g., "ship" or "airplane".

Be sure to note the scroll bar, which is unfortunately a bit inconspicuous, or even better, enlarge the window at its edges.

Overview about the categories:

Images	Icons	Cutout People	Stickers	Illustrations	Cartoon-People

- New from Office 2024 are the videos, which can be easily inserted into a presentation and can be resized and moved like a rectangle

- If you want to import your own pictures, it helps if these pictures are in an easy-to-find folder, e.g., C:\Photos.

8.2 CHANGE INDENT

As described on page 19, you can move or indent the entire paragraph by moving the text box. If paragraphs are to be set up very differently, it is best to put them in different text fields.

If you have inserted a wide bullet point or a small picture, it can happen that the indentation is too small. Then the paragraph can be set appropriately in the ruler.

> If the ruler is not activated, switch it on with View/Ruler.

> Enlarge the presentation.

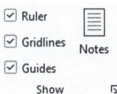

Now you can use the sliders in the ruler to change the paragraph indent:

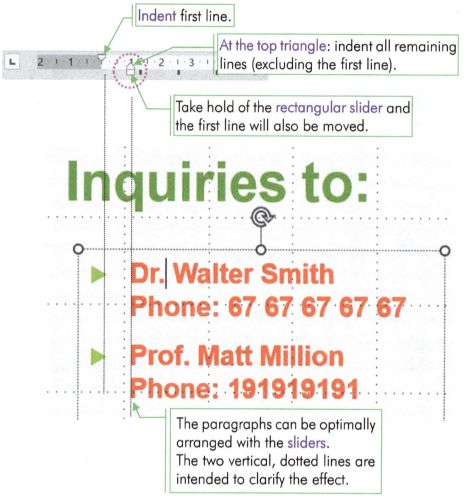

Indent first line.

At the top triangle: indent all remaining lines (excluding the first line).

Take hold of the rectangular slider and the first line will also be moved.

The paragraphs can be optimally arranged with the sliders.
The two vertical, dotted lines are intended to clarify the effect.

♦ Each change only applies to the current text box, including all paragraphs it contains!

   ✥ If you want to set different paragraphs in a text field, you should assign different outline levels (list levels) or use two different text boxes.

You may have wondered about the strange little bars under the ruler:

These small bars show the default tab stops defined for each paragraph.

♦ Since these apply to every paragraph, the standard tab stops can also be set in the paragraph menu (right mouse button/paragraph or click the expansion arrow for paragraph), then go to Tabs:

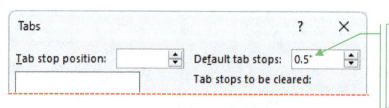

If you use centimeters: The default setting 1.27cm = ½ inch is not suitable for centimeter units, so change it to 2 cm, for example.

8.3 VARY PARAGRAPH SPACING

To get to the menu to increase or decrease the paragraph and line spacing, do the following: right-click on the paragraph, then Paragraph..., whereby you can also select several paragraphs at once to set them together:

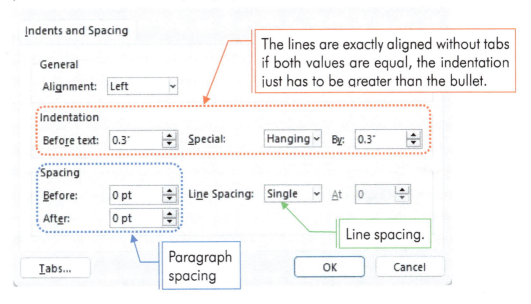

For paragraph spacing, indentation and special indentation:

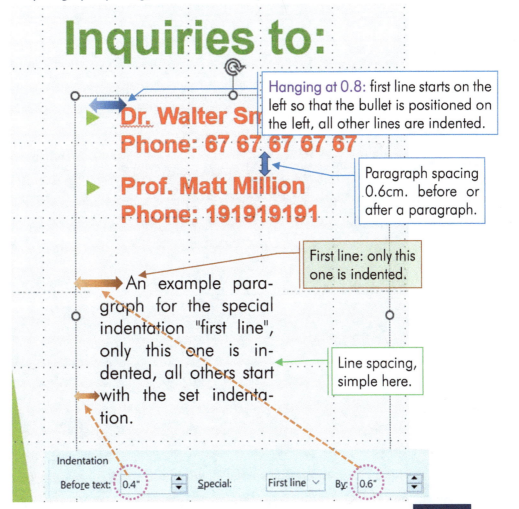

9. TABS

Tabs allow us to align text in different paragraphs with each other. That would make sense for our phone numbers if the list were longer.

First, let's practice copying a page as a template:

➤ Mark the entire last page in the outline view on the left by pressing the page symbol (4 or preview),

➤ then copy and paste to create a new page:

> In practice, you can also accept the default paragraphs and graphics in this way and only overwrite the texts.

Now we have the page duplicate so we can practice with the tabs, after practice delete one page so that the nicer version remains.

➤ Delete the line break so that both name and phone number are placed on one line.

➤ If available, delete the blue example paragraph and add three more example addresses instead.

Inquiries to:
   * Dr Walter Smith, Phone: 67 67 67 67 67
   * Prof. Dr Matt Million, Phone: 099/999 999 999
   * Karl Moos, Phone: 191919191
   * Anton Steel, Phone: 234 2345
   * Son Deng Weng, Phone: 7754332
   * Urs Hell, Phone: 33 22 566

➤ Mark all paragraphs (click + [Ctrl]-a), reset all settings with [Ctrl]-Spacebar,

➤ then right-click on the marking, then select Font and set the same color and a slightly smaller font.

9.1 ABOUT TABS

We will now practice using the tabs.

There are two steps to creating a tab:

♦ In the text, a tabulator must be set in front of "Phone:" in each line with the tabulator key.

♦ The position for this tabulator can then be specified in the ruler.

Of course, several tabs can also be installed.

9.2 SET TABS

Now we can set a tab in the ruler:

➢ Show this with View/Ruler if the ruler is not visible.

➢ Put a tab in front of each "Phone:" with the tabulator key, but delete the comma after each name.

☑ Ruler
☑ Gridlines
☑ Guides
Show

First, an important note about tabs:

> All paragraphs must be marked in order for the tabulator to be set for all paragraphs.

➢ After marking, set and arrange the tab in the ruler.

Click in the ruler to set a tab. The tabulator can then be moved with the mouse.

Inquiries to:

> ➢ Dr Walter Smith   Phone: 67 67 67 67 67
>
> ➢ Prof. Matt Million   Phone: 191 919 191
>
> ➢ Albert Onestone: Phone: 159 159 159
>
> ➢ James Smith: Phone: 445 556 444
>
> ➢ Donald Truck: Phone: 984 984 984 984
>
> ➢ Emily Sanders: Phone: 19 11 11 85 55

If you have placed a tab in front of "Phone:", all "Phone:" will be aligned with the tab.

How do we get the fill character?

♦ Unfortunately, no filler characters (in this example the underline) can be set in PowerPoint like in MS Word.

↳ However, we can delete the space bar, then mark the tabulator with the [Shift] key pressed and the right direction key once and simply underline it.

In a real list, which is usually much more extensive, these changes would be very labor-intensive by hand. In MS Word we could use "Search and Replace" to find the comma + space bar + tab and replace it with a tab, unfortunately the replace function in PowerPoint does not offer this functionality, since PowerPoint pages are usually only short.

> No problem, for short texts: set the first tabulator underlined, mark and copy and paste it manually in the following correctly formatted, for longer texts: copy the text, paste it into Word, make the changes there with "Search and Replace" and back to PowerPoint copy.

More about tabs:

♦ You can switch between different tabs by pressing the icon on the far left of the ruler:
left justified, centered, right justified, decimal.

[L] ↳ left-justified: the text is arranged on the left below one another,

[⊥] ↳ centered: the text is aligned to the middle of the text,

[⌐] ↳ right-aligned: the text is aligned to the right,

[⊥.] ↳ decimal: for numbers, prices, etc., because the dot is always one below the other.

Decimal tabs are good for pricing because the dot aligns with each other.

Deleting tabs:

♦ You can delete tabs by dragging them out of the ruler while holding down the mouse button and then releasing the mouse button.

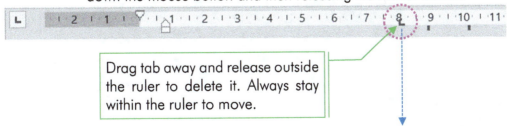

Drag tab away and release outside the ruler to delete it. Always stay within the ruler to move.

➢ Delete the previously copied page to be on the safe side, now page 4: click on the thumbnail or 4 and press [Del].

10. PAGE SETUP, PRINT

> ➤ Choose Design/Slide Size/Custom Slide Size...

Here you can select various presetting's for the page size, e.g., overhead or widescreen or letter or enter the desired dimensions manually.

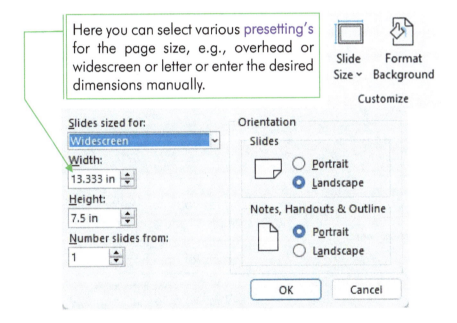

Notes on the page format:

- ◆ PowerPoint does a lot automatically. For example, if you choose a different format, PowerPoint automatically adjusts the font size so that the slide as a whole remains largely unchanged.

  - ✇ Try this out by setting a small page format, e.g., 6x4 in, and comparing the font size before and after.

  - ✇ For this reason, the settings for the page format in PowerPoint are irrelevant unless the presentation is to be printed out.

  - ✇ The slide show is set up for a 15-inch monitor, for example, but is enlarged accordingly to full screen on each screen.

- ◆ If you switch to A4 (21x29.7 cm), the default is 27.52 x 19.05 cm. You can see the missing centimeters on 29.7x21 cm as a margin. The slide is adjusted accordingly when you print it out.

It is a good idea to try printing right away so that you can see that the default settings for the page format are not critical here either.

10.1 PRINTING

As in almost every program, you can open the print menu with the command File/Print or the shortcut [Ctrl]-P.

In the print menu that appears, you can specify exactly what is to be printed and how.

- ♦ At the top under Printer, click the "Printer Properties" button to access your printer's menu.
  - ✍ These menus vary by printer.
  - ✍ With inkjet printers, it is very important to select the type of paper used and the desired print quality.

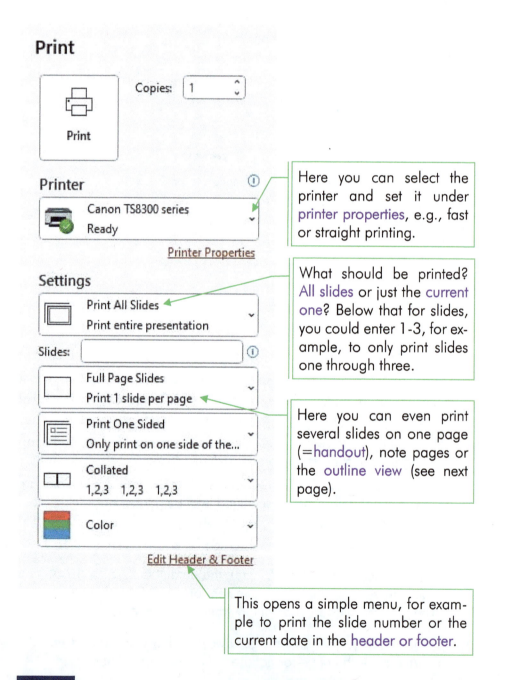

Here you can select the printer and set it under printer properties, e.g., fast or straight printing.

What should be printed? All slides or just the current one? Below that for slides, you could enter 1-3, for example, to only print slides one through three.

Here you can even print several slides on one page (=handout), note pages or the outline view (see next page).

This opens a simple menu, for example to print the slide number or the current date in the header or footer.

10.2 SLIDES OR HANDOUTS

If you click by "Full Page Slides", you find these options:

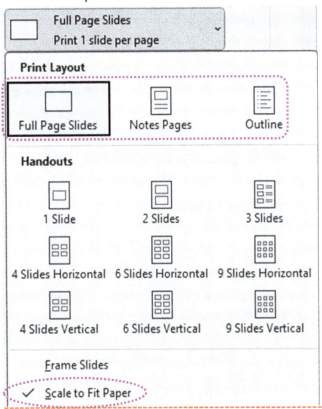

♦ With "Full Page Slides", you can print the slides with background and font formatting as set.

♦ With Handouts, you can automatically reduce multiple slides to one or more sheets of paper. This is good for overviews.

☞ You can only specify how many slides are to be fitted onto a sheet of paper for handouts.

♦ "Scale to Fit Paper" allows you to print as large as possible to fit the currently selected setting.

♦ "Notes Pages" are used to print one slide at a time, which can be used as a supporting sheet for the speaker.

♦ Handouts: several slides can be printed on one sheet in a reduced size, simply select the desired number.

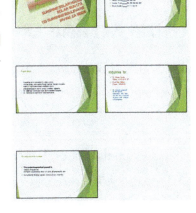

➢ Try note pages with 6 slides vertical and print this.

♦ When selecting "Outline", only the contained text is printed without frames, graphics and background colors:

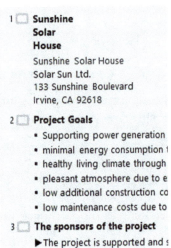

1 □ **Sunshine Solar House**

Sunshine Solar House
Solar Sun Ltd.
133 Sunshine Boulevard
Irvine, CA 92618

2 □ **Project Goals**

• Supporting power generation
• minimal energy consumption
• healthy living climate through
• pleasant atmosphere due to e
• low additional construction co
• low maintenance costs due to

3 □ **The sponsors of the project**

▶ The project is supported and s
• Solar-Sun Example Ltd.,

10.3 THE PREVIEW

The print preview, which you can see in the print menu on the right, is very practical and highly recommended. In the print preview you can see exactly what would be printed and how.

You can also rely on this display so that, for example, if everything was only displayed in black and white, you can assume that only a black and white printer was selected or that the color button was accidentally switched to grayscale.

Therefore, if something is not optimal in the preview, it is better to start troubleshooting first than to print.

10.3.1 PRINT MENU

When you have printed, the printer symbol appears in the start bar at the bottom right:

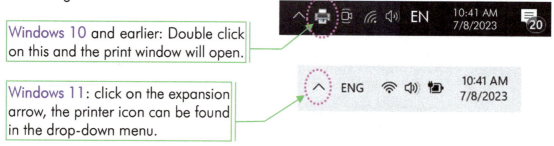

Windows 10 and earlier: Double click on this and the print window will open.

Windows 11: click on the expansion arrow, the printer icon can be found in the drop-down menu.

- ♦ In the print menu you can mark print jobs and then delete or stop them.

- ♦ This print symbol disappears automatically as soon as the print has been completely forwarded to the printer.

10.4 SETTING UP THE SLIDE SHOW

➢ As soon as you press the "Slide Show" button at the bottom right, the presentation starts.

Before that, let's look at the slide show preferences.

➢ You can open the settings menu at any time in the Slide Show Menu with the "Set Up Slide Show" command.

A simple and self-explanatory menu starts:

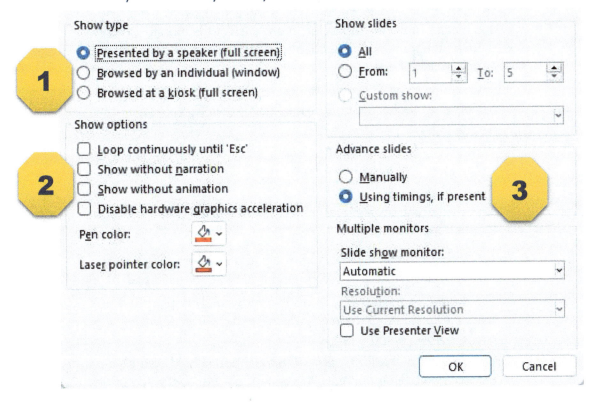

To the settings:

1. ♦ You can specify the *type of presentation*, such as full screen if it is a real performance,
   - ↳ which is also recommended for a presentation via beamer or television,

2. ♦ a desired automatic *repeat*,
   - ↳ If you select *"Browsed at a kiosk"*, this is preset so that the presentation runs overnight in the shop window, for example,

3. ♦ the control *manual or automatic*: if a display duration is available, the next slide is selected after this, otherwise manually.
   - ↳ Chapter 15.8 on page 86 explains how a *display duration* can be specified.

Some tips:

♦ *Reducing the resolution* is useful if, for example, you use a good 4K monitor (3840x2160) on your PC, but want to show the presentation to the customer on your laptop with only HD = 1920x1080 points resolution or on a projector with only 720x576 points resolution.

- ↳ You see the presentation identically when you create it on the PC as later on the presentation device.

- If you want the presentation to run automatically, for example in a shop window or at a trade fair, you should deactivate the energy saving functions of your computer, in any case of the monitor, to prevent the screen from being switched off after a period of non-use and of course switch off the screen saver.
  - ↬ This can be done in Windows with the right mouse button on the Windows symbol at the bottom left, then Power Options (Windows 10 and 11).
  - ↬ With other Windows versions, usually the standard way: Start/Settings, go to System and then Power and "Screen and sleep", deactivate the screen switch-off here.
  - ↬ Test whether the presentation really is not switched off even after a longer period of time.

- You should also prevent viewers from being able to stop the presentation if they have access to the PC at a trade fair, for example.
  - ↬ The easiest and safest way to do this is to simply unplug and put away the keyboard and mouse, which is not a problem when using a USB keyboard and mouse.
  - ↬ It is more difficult with a laptop; the touchpad should also be deactivated here. Unfortunately, this can usually be reactivated using special keys, so the laptop keyboard should also be deactivated.
  - ↬ You can then activate it again using either a USB mouse or an external USB keyboard, which of course should be provided and tested in advance.

For the demonstration:

- Set the brightness and contrast optimally according to the lighting conditions. Never turn up the brightness too much, always increase the contrast as much as possible first.

- Always carry out a test for important presentations to ensure that the monitors, the music and the controls work, that the operation is clear and that everything is optimally preset.
  - ↬ If something doesn't work during a demonstration in the presence of the customers, a stressful situation quickly arises in which even banal causes of error such as hidden main switches or remote controls hidden in drawers or unplugged plugs cannot be found.
  - ↬ Therefore, if possible, always test exactly as in the real presentation, i.e., in the demonstration room and with the equipment available there.
  - ↬ Otherwise, for example, an unfamiliar mouse with any scroll functions can lead to unexpected problems during the presentation or because someone has defined some keyboard shortcuts on the PC that is there.

3rd Section

THEME, BACKGROUND, ANIMATIONS

Gradient Text Boxes, set the Background, Apply the Theme, the Animations

11. TEXT BOXES WITH BACKGROUND

We'll stick with the previous exercise, because there are still a few things that can be adjusted to make it even nicer.

11.1 TEXT BOX WITH LINE AND FILL

In the previous chapter you saw that text is arranged in text frames. This means that the text can not only be arranged as you wish, but this text frame can also be assigned an individual filling and line color, just like with graphic objects.

> ➢ Right-click on a text box and select "Format Shape" from the drop-down menu.

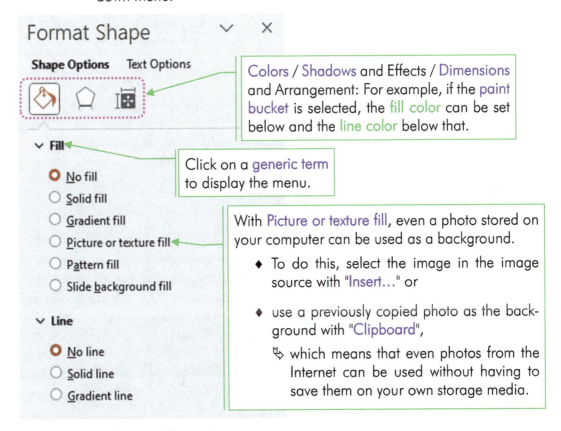

In the case of "Pattern fill", many prefabricated patterns can be selected, e.g., slanted lines, dots or a checkerboard pattern. In the case of "Slide background fill", the text frame is simply not filled as with "No fill" so that the fill of the slide is visible.

11.2 COLORED FILL

➢ Select the item "Solid fill".

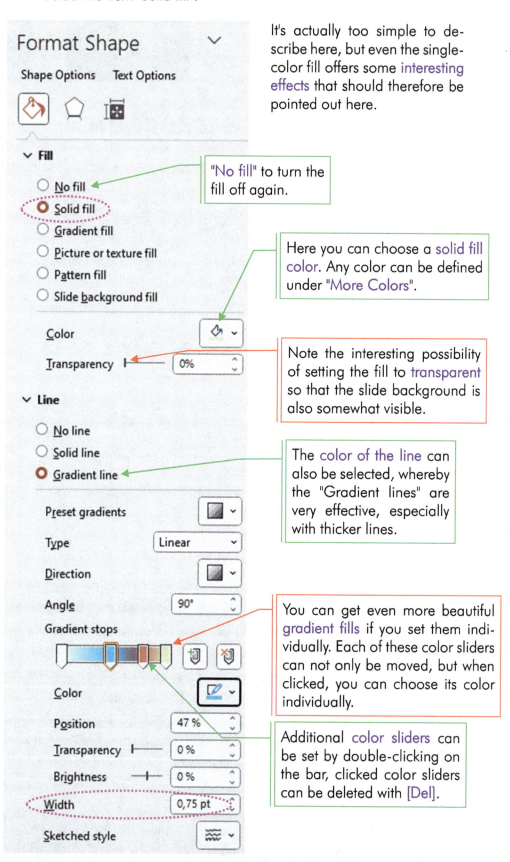

It's actually too simple to describe here, but even the single-color fill offers some interesting effects that should therefore be pointed out here.

"No fill" to turn the fill off again.

Here you can choose a solid fill color. Any color can be defined under "More Colors".

Note the interesting possibility of setting the fill to transparent so that the slide background is also somewhat visible.

The color of the line can also be selected, whereby the "Gradient lines" are very effective, especially with thicker lines.

You can get even more beautiful gradient fills if you set them individually. Each of these color sliders can not only be moved, but when clicked, you can choose its color individually.

Additional color sliders can be set by double-clicking on the bar, clicked color sliders can be deleted with [Del].

Example of a frame with transparency and gradient line:

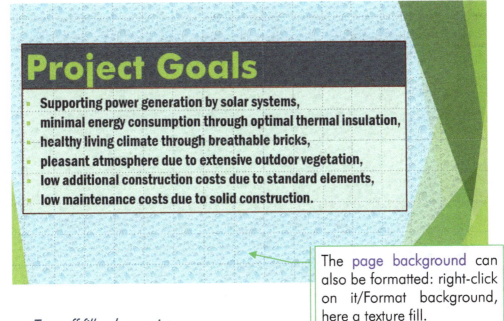

The page background can also be formatted: right-click on it/Format background, here a texture fill.

Turn off fill color again:

♦ Note that you can switch off the filling with "No fill" at any time.

    ↳ The frame is then transparent, the background is visible,

    ↳ while with the fill color "white" the frame would be filled white and what is behind it would be covered.

11.3 LOCATION AND SIZE

If we give the text frame a colored background and thus make it clearly visible, it is more important that the text is arranged correctly, e.g., vertically centered and horizontally in the middle.

♦ This can be set at the top right with "Text Options/Text-field":

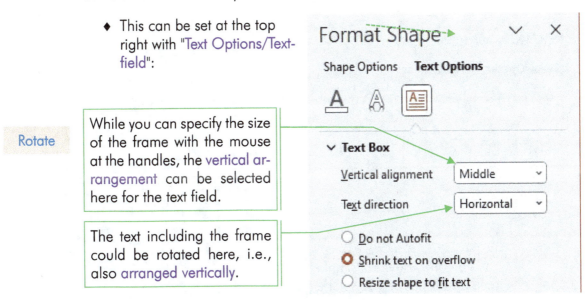

Rotate

While you can specify the size of the frame with the mouse at the handles, the vertical arrangement can be selected here for the text field.

The text including the frame could be rotated here, i.e., also arranged vertically.

♦ The horizontal arrangement of the text can be selected as usual at "Home", e.g., left-aligned or centered.

11.3.1 THE SIZE OF THE TEXT BOX

The distance between the frame and the text it contains can also be specified for text fields, and whether the frame size should adapt to the text or the text on the frame:

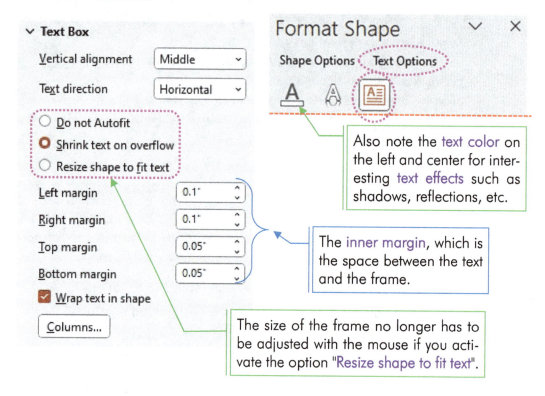

11.3.2 THE PATTERN FILL

You can only use these simple patterns properly if you set the colors optimally, whereby the foreground and background color can be chosen.

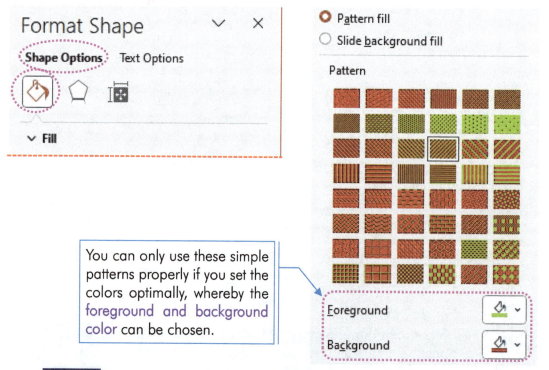

12. SLIDE BACKGROUND

In the previous chapter we set the text frames. Of course, the actual background can also be modified or a completely different scheme can be selected. Sequentially.

12.1 OVERVIEW SLIDE SETTINGS

With the following method we can set the main color of the background.

> Choose Design/Format Background or press the right mouse button on the background (=not on a text field or text), then you have the following options.

Overview:

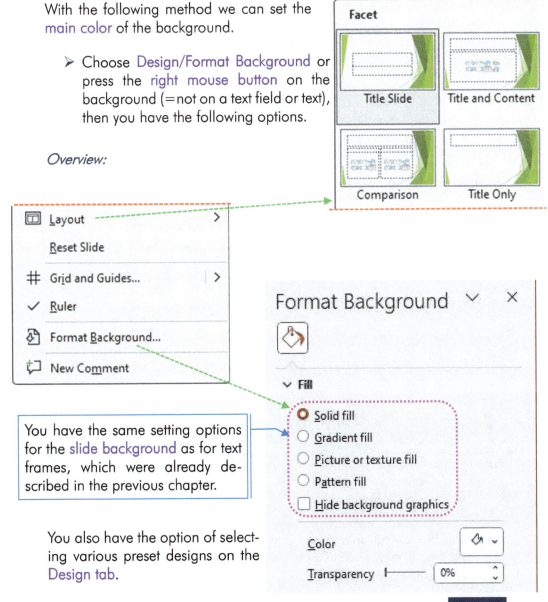

You have the same setting options for the slide background as for text frames, which were already described in the previous chapter.

You also have the option of selecting various preset designs on the Design tab.

12.1.1 RIGHT MOUSE BUTTON OR ON DESIGN

Difference between the Design tab and the right mouse button:

♦ Foil design on the Design tab: select various color combinations for fonts, backgrounds and effects.

♦ Right mouse button/Layout: as shown on the previous page, templates for differently arranged text frames can be selected.

♦ Format Background, accessible by right-clicking as shown on the previous page or from the Design menu:

Format Background

  ✍ The color of the background can be set in this menu.

  ✍ Color gradients or patterns can be selected in addition to a monochrome background.

12.1.2 RESET BACKGROUND OR APPLY TO ALL?

On the previous page, at the bottom of the "Format Background" menu, notice the option to apply the settings to all slides instead of just the current slide:

If you've tried several colors and don't want to go all the way back to the master slide preset, you can also use Undo to go back command by command.

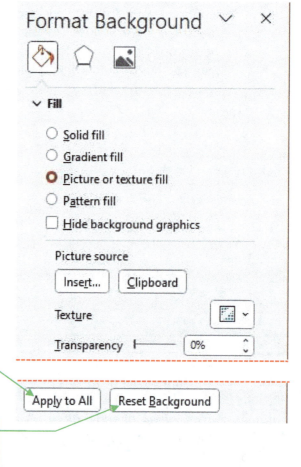

For the current slide only or for all?

Return to the preset (master slide).

The biggest advantage of this menu is the option to "Apply to All", i.e., to all slides in this presentation, since a uniform design from start to finish is usually desired.

♦ You will also find the item "Hide background graphics" in this filling menu. Each slide is based on a so-called master slide, whose settings are initially adopted.

    ↳ If there are graphics on the master slide, you can use this to hide them on the current slide.

12.2 SELECT SLIDE DESIGN

On the Design tab you have many more setting options than with the right mouse button.

♦ On the far left the Themes, preset slides with different graphics and colors:

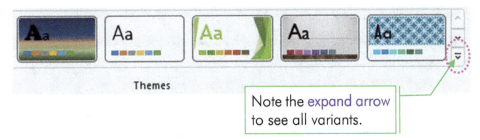

Note the expand arrow to see all variants.

♦ Then the Variants follow, here different color combinations can be selected for the chosen design:

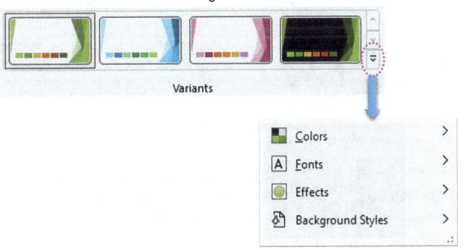

♦ Colors: presets and the option to choose them manually.

♦ Fonts: these are changed here for all frames, unless a frame's font has already been manually set, and "Apply to All" could set the fonts on all slides in one action. So, if possible, do not set fonts manually (click frame and select font), but use this.

♦ Effects: the colors can be brighter or darker, the shapes can be set with shadows or soft edges, for example.

♦ Background Styles: the background color can be set here, which can therefore be seen everywhere if there are no graphic elements in front of it.

12.3 ARRANGE PERFECTLY

With the right mouse button/layout you can choose a different layout of the frames if you don't click on an element but on the background. This can be used to set different text frames for individual slides, because the change only applies to the current slide. However, this is usually faster manually.

♦ Text boxes can already be moved or resized with the mouse.

♦ A new text frame can be drawn with the Insert/Text Box command while holding down the mouse button.

  ✍ Write text in the frame immediately before you move it or want to change the size, as an empty frame is automatically hidden.

The following useful commands can be found on the View menu:

♦ The ruler for indenting paragraphs was introduced in the tabs exercise on page 35.

♦ You can also activate or deactivate the grid lines and guide lines in the View menu:

  ✍ Grid lines: thin, dotted lines at 100% at a distance of approx. 1.8 cm, which are usually no longer recognizable on a colored background, but only on a white background, and to which objects are not aligned by default. So, we have to adjust them better first.

  ✍ Guide lines: Auxiliary lines, of which any number can be inserted both horizontally and vertically and to which objects are aligned: automatic exact docking as soon as they are close by when moving or changing size.

Set grid and guidelines by View:

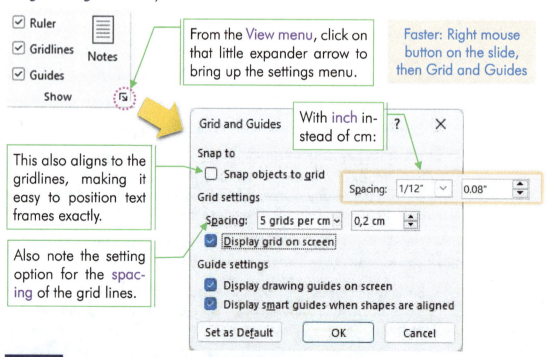

From the View menu, click on that little expander arrow to bring up the settings menu.

Faster: Right mouse button on the slide, then Grid and Guides

This also aligns to the gridlines, making it easy to position text frames exactly.

Also note the setting option for the spacing of the grid lines.

With inch instead of cm:

Set the spacing for the grid:　　　　*With inch instead of cm*

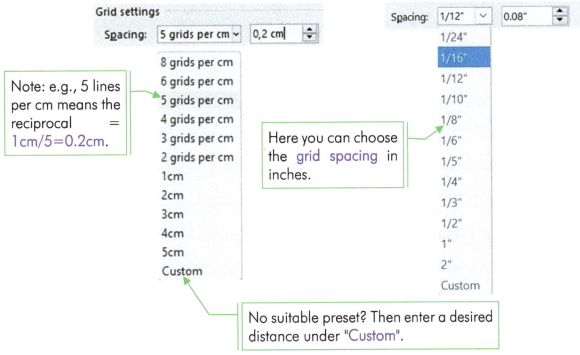

Note: e.g., 5 lines per cm means the reciprocal = 1cm/5=0.2cm.

Here you can choose the grid spacing in inches.

No suitable preset? Then enter a desired distance under "Custom".

Add more guides:

♦ This works best with the right mouse button (=not on a text field or text), then grid and guides…:

  ♆ Here you can insert both horizontal and vertical guide lines and then move them to the desired position with the mouse.

♦ If we first set that objects are also automatically arranged along the grid lines, this also applies to newly inserted guide lines.

  ♆ Elements can then be arranged relatively easily with the mouse at exactly the same height.

The menu with right mouse button:

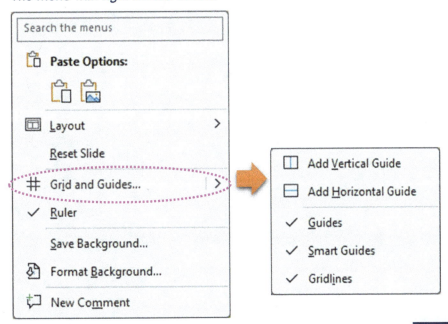

13. THE ANIMATIONS

Now that we've enhanced the presentation graphically, here are some amazing ways to make the presentation more impactful. With the animations you can emphasize particularly important things and increase the attention of the viewers.

> By means of an animation, the text is e.g., faded in when the slide is opened, tumbles in from above or is reinforced by a flashlight or as if written by a typewriter.

♦ When text or a text frame is selected, you can select the following effects for animations:

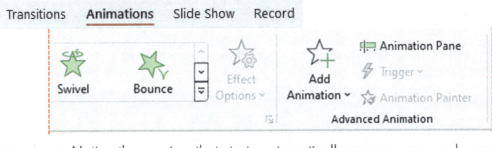

Preview

⌄

Preview

♦ Notice the preview that starts automatically as soon as you choose another animation or when you click the Preview button.

↻ These animations apply to the text paragraphs, you can set something similar for the slide change on the Transitions tab.

Adjust animation, e.g., the speed.

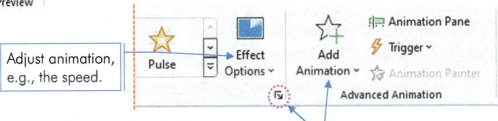

To the full menu with all animations and settings, here you can also add other effects to an animation. By the way, the symbol and the expansion arrow open the same menu.

➢ Assign some animations to the text blocks and examine the result using the preview.

13.1 SET ANIMATIONS

♦ In the effect options you can choose the direction and sequence (= simultaneously or each paragraph one after the other).

Depending on which animation was assigned, other or no setting options are available.

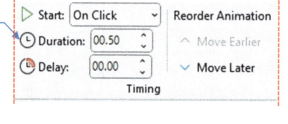

13.2 SET TIMING

♦ You can set the speed and the start event directly on the Animations tab on the right:

Duration: the time in which the animation runs, shorter = faster. Delay = a waiting time before the animation starts.

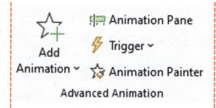

♦ Also notice the Trigger button, because here you can specify how the animation is started, e.g., by clicking on Title or Content.

You can change the order using the arrow buttons, which of course is only possible once there are several animations on one page:

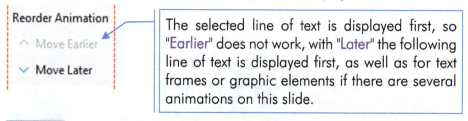

The selected line of text is displayed first, so "Earlier" does not work, with "Later" the following line of text is displayed first, as well as for text frames or graphic elements if there are several animations on this slide.

13.2.1 THE ANIMATION AREA

This area is a help for viewing and setting the timing. When you click the icon, a window will appear on the right showing all the animations present on the current slide.

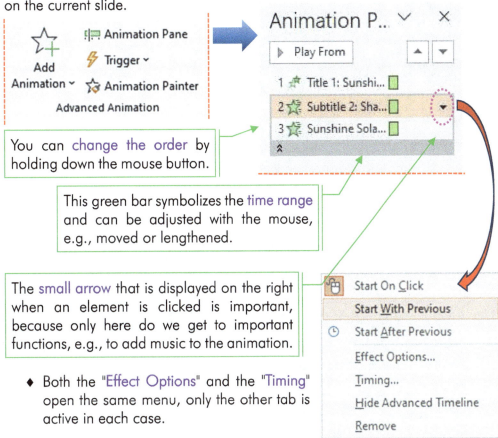

You can change the order by holding down the mouse button.

This green bar symbolizes the time range and can be adjusted with the mouse, e.g., moved or lengthened.

The small arrow that is displayed on the right when an element is clicked is important, because only here do we get to important functions, e.g., to add music to the animation.

♦ Both the "Effect Options" and the "Timing" open the same menu, only the other tab is active in each case.

Here you can now set everything in terms of time:

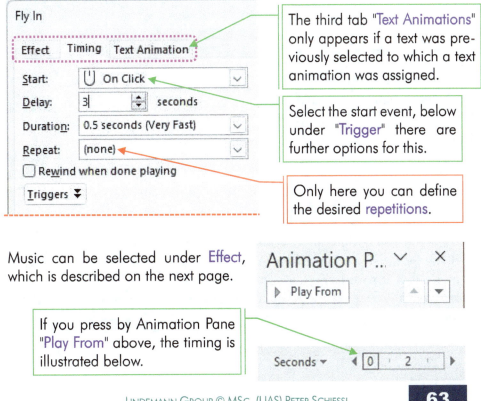

The third tab "Text Animations" only appears if a text was previously selected to which a text animation was assigned.

Select the start event, below under "Trigger" there are further options for this.

Only here you can define the desired repetitions.

Music can be selected under Effect, which is described on the next page.

If you press by Animation Pane "Play From" above, the timing is illustrated below.

On the Text Animation tab, you will find the option of running the animation in reverse order, as well as the option of starting the animation automatically after a certain waiting time, i.e., without having to click.

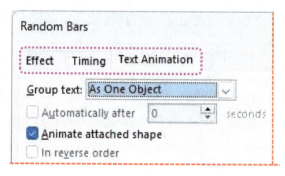

13.3 ADD SOUND

> Good "sound" is the key to a lasting impression and turns a dry performance into an experience. Optimal only with surround speakers and subwoofer for the bass.

You can also assign music to an animation on the Effect tab (see previous page), but there are other options hidden here, e.g., to fade in the text word by word or to fade out after the effect.

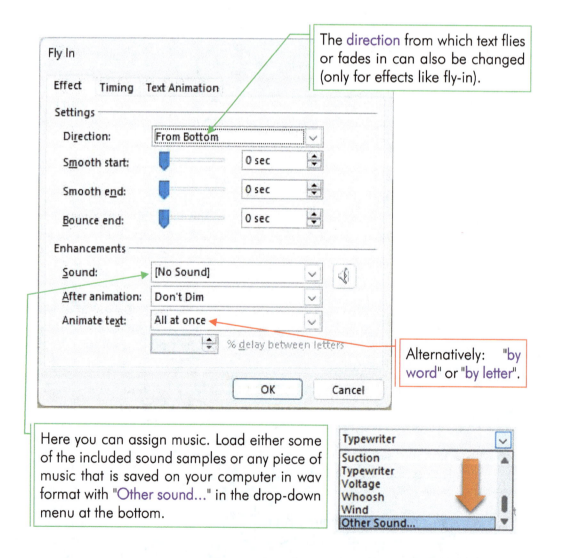

The direction from which text flies or fades in can also be changed (only for effects like fly-in).

Alternatively: "by word" or "by letter".

Here you can assign music. Load either some of the included sound samples or any piece of music that is saved on your computer in wav format with "Other sound..." in the drop-down menu at the bottom.

For further settings under "Enhancements":

- ♦ "Dim" on "After animation:" will fade the text out once the effect is over, which is rarely desirable.

- ♦ Animate Text: With "By Word" isn't quite as quick, since the current effect is applied to one word before the next, with "By letter", letter-by-letter.

- ➢ Try other animation compilations.

13.4 THE ANIMATION PAINTER

This is a handy feature similar to MS Word Format Painter. When you've got an animation optimally tuned, you can paint (copy) the exact same animation to other text boxes by clicking the finished text box, choosing the "Animation Painter", and then clicking the destination box.

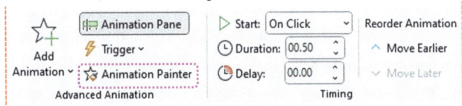

- ♦ If you want to transfer an animation to several text fields, select the finished text frame and activate this function by double-clicking on "Animation Painter" until you double-click on "Animation Painter" again.

Notes: ....

....

....

....

....

....

....

....

....

....

....

....

4th Section

CLIPART AND SOUNDS

Find and insert clipart, clip gallery and organizer, integrate music, control presentation

14. PRESENTATION WITH GRAPHICS

Now we're going to create a presentation from scratch. We will create the various elements that make up a presentation by hand:

- ♦ A background slide with the background and graphic elements,

- ♦ multiple outline pages for the different slides and

- ♦ Text frames, which determine the arrangement of the text on the slides.

In addition, we can make the pages more effective with animations.

14.1 NEW PRESENTATION

Let's start from scratch.

- ➤ In PowerPoint, choose File/New, then "Blank Presentation".

- ♦ You could now choose a design template for the Design tab, but with daily professional use, the given designs are quickly used and thus worn out.

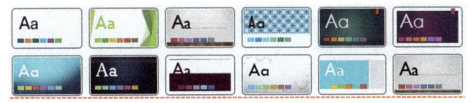

- ♦ Or you could choose a pattern in Home/Layout with one text frame for the title and two for the text and image below, e.g., "two content".

> But this time, let's learn how to set up a slide. So, we don't use help, we do everything manually.

14.2 STYLE PAGE

We want to create a letter sheet in landscape format that can later be printed on paper and posted.

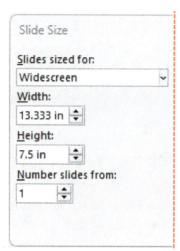

> ➤ If necessary, delete existing text frames (click on the line and [Del]).

> ➤ Under Design/Slide Size, select a "Custom Slide Size..." corresponding to letter or DIN A4, landscape. Confirm the message that appears, we don't have any elements yet.

It is now important to set the grid correctly next, so that the frame and auxiliary lines are aligned with it and are therefore positioned exactly.

> ➤ Click on the expansion arrow under View/Show and, since we have a fairly large format, also enter more distant grid spacing, and activate "Snap objects to grid".

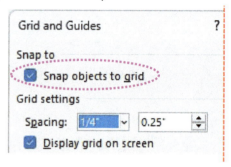

> ➤ Now you can easily drag two text frames (Insert/Text Box) that are exactly aligned, one for the title, one below on the left for the text, on the right we will then insert a photo.

As a suggestion:

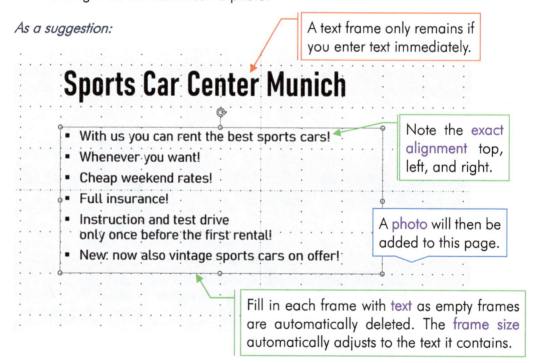

A text frame only remains if you enter text immediately.

Sports Car Center Munich

- With us you can rent the best sports cars!
- Whenever you want!
- Cheap weekend rates!
- Full insurance!
- Instruction and test drive only once before the first rental!
- New: now also vintage sports cars on offer!

Note the exact alignment top, left, and right.

A photo will then be added to this page.

Fill in each frame with text as empty frames are automatically deleted. The frame size automatically adjusts to the text it contains.

Note: You can always choose a different design. Existing text frames with text will not be deleted if you switch to a template with fewer frames. To be on the safe side, save beforehand and, if necessary, undo or close immediately without saving.

14.3 IMPORT GRAPHICS

A picture is needed! First an overview:

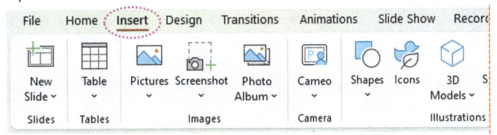

♦ Pictures: you can use this to insert photos from your computer or from the Internet.

♦ Screenshot: create a photo of your monitor, select either an open window or screen section from the drop-down menu, then mark a rectangular area with the mouse button pressed.

♦ Photo album: here you can select photos that will be placed in a photo album, but this photo presentation will not run in a frame of your current project, but a new presentation will be opened.

    ✎ This command is incorrectly sorted here under "Paste", because nothing is pasted into the current project.

♦ It's best to take a look for yourself: Shapes (simple graphics such as rectangles, stars...), icons (small black and white images), 3D Models (three-dimensionally drawn elements), SmartArt (flow charts) and Charts (the data table will be the same included and can be overwritten).

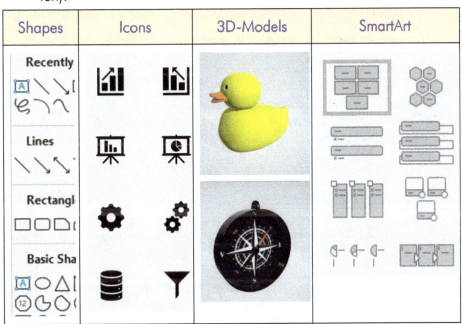

♦ On the far right of the Insert menu you can add videos, again either from your computer or online, and audios or record them from your screen, e.g., create a section of a YouTube video that you are currently playing on your screen and hereby record it.

14.4 SEARCH IMAGES

An overview of the options for finding images:

♦ If you use the Insert/Pictures/Online Pictures... function, you will get a clear selection of certain keywords based on search hits from the Microsoft search engine "bing".

♦ Of course, you can also search the Internet using a search engine of your choice.

    ✎ Then temporarily save the desired photos, videos or sound sources on your hard drive and insert them into your PowerPoint presentation via Insert/Pictures/This device....

    ✎ Of course, you are responsible for observing the relevant copyrights.

♦ You can also search your hard drive or a DVD that has just been inserted for pictures, music or videos.

    ✎ A number of treasures are hidden on many CDs/DVDs, e.g., images provided with programs or some free clip art on CDs enclosed with computer magazines.

    ✎ To do this, select the desired drive in Windows Explorer, e.g., hard disk C:\ or DVD drive, and enter a search word in the search button at the top right, e.g., cars.

You can also generally search directly for photos, videos or pieces of music without a search name using the file extension:

♦ "*.jpg" for photos in jpg format, most photos are saved in this format, only a few in other formats such as "*.gif", "*.bmp", "*.tiff" or "*.png".

♦ "*.wav" for digital or *.mp3 for compressed music or

♦ enter "*.avi" or "*.mpg" for videos.

> The "*" stands for any file name, followed by the file extension for the desired file type.

Insert photo into the presentation:

➢ Search the Internet for two sports car photos and save them to your local storage device.

➢ Insert a 3D model in the middle, e.g., a dragon (Insert/3D Models/Stock 3D models/Fantasy) and two sports cars on the right with Insert/Pictures/Online Pictures.

    ✎ Click on each image and use the handles that appear to make it smaller, paying attention to how the images are based on the grid.

    ✎ More on adjustment and arrangement on the next page.

14.5 EDITING IMAGES

We have two problems with sports cars. On the one hand, the format doesn't fit, we actually need a picture in portrait format, which is rarely the case with a car, and on the other hand, the background is usually annoying, we almost only want to see the sports cars.

A possible and simple solution: we simply insert two sports car images, reduce them, rotate each image a little and place the two images on top of each other so that the space with portrait format is largely filled, and we reduce the background with the effect "Soft Edges".

Illustrative example (search for similar photos):

Proceeding:

> ➤ Insert the sport car photos, click and resize the corner handles while holding down the mouse button. Note the mark in the photo above, also for the spin arrow.

> ➤ There is a rotating handle in the top center, you can use this to rotate the photo.

> ➤ With the right mouse button/in the foreground or background you can adjust the order optimally.

> ➤ If you click on a graphic element, the appropriate command appears at the top of the PowerPoint, e.g., picture format or shape format.

> ↳ Click on "Picture Format" in the command bar on the right it to show the commands for graphic editing.

> ↳ There you will find the "Soft edges" effect in the "Picture Effects", with which you can easily hide the background to a large extent.

14.6 GRAPHIC AND IMAGE PROCESSING

♦ Also, when you click a graphic, you can click "Shape Format" at the top to bring up the graphic commands, which are slightly different than the photo commands:

Examples of symbols for photos by "Picture Format":

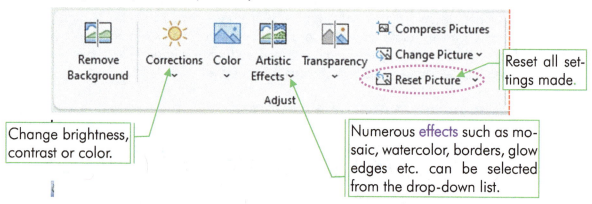

Change brightness, contrast or color.

Reset all settings made.

Numerous effects such as mosaic, watercolor, borders, glow edges etc. can be selected from the drop-down list.

♦ Compress Pictures: Reduce resolution or permanently delete cropped areas.

♦ Change Pictures: choose another photo. Even easier: delete this one and insert a new one.

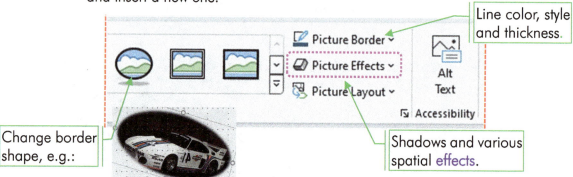

Line color, style and thickness.

Change border shape, e.g.:

Shadows and various spatial effects.

♦ Picture Layout: different layouts of the graphic with descriptive text can be selected. The graphic is often placed in a frame and cut off; this can be adjusted later with the mouse.

Rotate or mirror: useful if you want an exact angle of rotation, mirroring or 90° rotation, otherwise rotate the object with the mouse.

Combine several drawn elements into one object = Group. Only works if several graphic elements have been selected beforehand while holding down the [Shift] key.

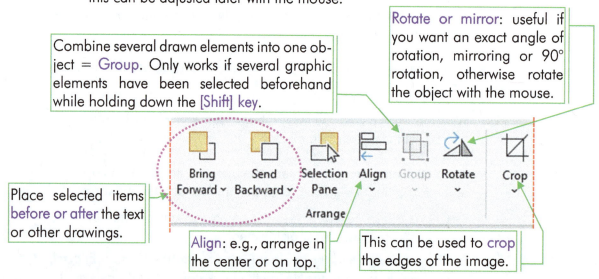

Place selected items before or after the text or other drawings.

Align: e.g., arrange in the center or on top.

This can be used to crop the edges of the image.

A text flow like in MS Word, whether the text flows around the graphic like in a newspaper or whether the text continues in front of or behind the graphic, e.g., to use the graphic as a background, does not exist in Power-Point to this day.

"Color" is where you'll find these interesting options:

♦ Thumbnails are displayed clearly and you can choose: lighter, darker, change the color tone or convert to black and white:

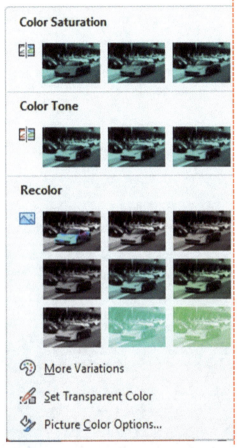

♦ More Variations: all colors are replaced by the selected color.

♦ Set Transparent Color: You can use the pipette to click on a color that is hidden, i.e., becomes transparent.

   ↳ This can be used, for example, to cut away an unwanted single-color background around an object.

   ↳ Only works for photos and only for one color tone, not for color gradients such as a sky that consists of different shades of blue.

♦ Picture Color Options…: the full menu opens, but some options are only available for photos, others for graphics.

♦ You can also use Windows Explorer and drag images from there.

14.7 NEW SLIDE

➢ Either with the icon or right click on the left side in the slide preview area, then "New Slide".

➢ Two text frames already exist, delete them, copy our title and text frames from the first slide here, the easiest method so that we have identical settings for font and frames.

➢ Since we only have one text frame on the first page, copy and paste it twice on the second slide, move the second one to the right side.

➢ Write an imaginary address in the right text field, then format the font appropriately and arrange the frame appropriately on the right side, see next figure.

14.8 SET BACKGROUND

➢ It's very easy. We use one of the many presets in Design/Themes.

↳ Note that you can manually adjust the colors of a theme as well as the colors of the text and the text frames.

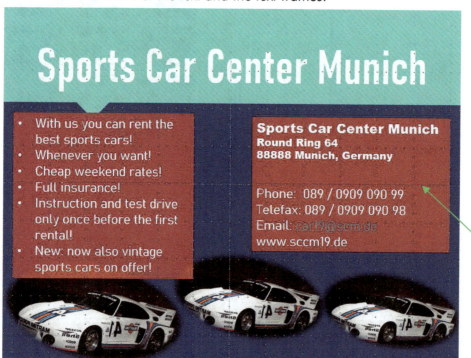

The frame for the address has been formatted individually:
- Right-click on the frame, then format shape.
- Here, the frame color was red, but a slight transparency was set (33%).
- The photo has been copied and pasted multiple times.

➢ Finally, arrange the images and text frames appropriately and experiment with the designs until you find a suitable one.

15. PRESENTATION CONTROLS

15.1 OTHER ANIMATIONS

Effects with sound add that certain something (see p. 64). Now we will perfect the music to the effects.

> ➤ Now assign animations to the text frame of the new Sport Car Center presentation, e.g., "Fly in".
>
>> ↳ If a text is not displayed in the menu, no animation has been assigned to it yet.
>
>> ↳ Since we want to assign animations to several objects, the Animation Pane helps to keep track.

If several texts are recorded, you can set the order of the effects with the arrow buttons.

> ➤ After an effect has been assigned and the text frame has been selected, you can set it in the "Effect Options", e.g. select "As Object" or "By Paragraph" - However, other options are available depending on the selected effect.

To the selection menu for all animations:

Click this expansion arrow to display all animations.

> Now notice the division into entrance, emphasis and exit effects in the menu.

To the effect setting menu:

> In the full menu you can find interesting setting options, e.g. char-
> acter by character or word by word, the respective delay time and a
> sound could be added.

➤ You can open the full menu with all animations by pressing the expansion arrow next to the animations.

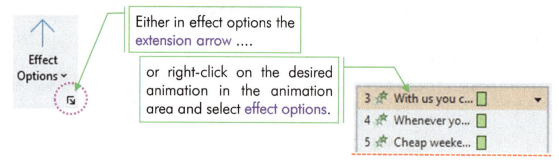

Either in effect options the extension arrow ....

or right-click on the desired animation in the animation area and select effect options.

Depending on the selected effect, other setting options are available:

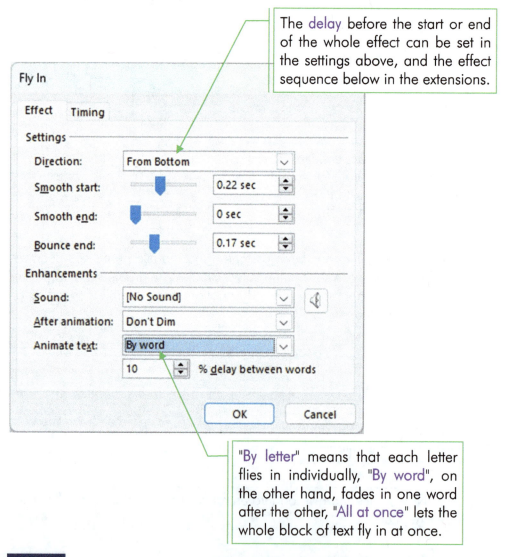

The delay before the start or end of the whole effect can be set in the settings above, and the effect sequence below in the extensions.

"By letter" means that each letter flies in individually, "By word", on the other hand, fades in one word after the other, "All at once" lets the whole block of text fly in at once.

15.2 ADD SOUND

When you have arranged the texts in the correct order, you can select the animations. There are even more options.

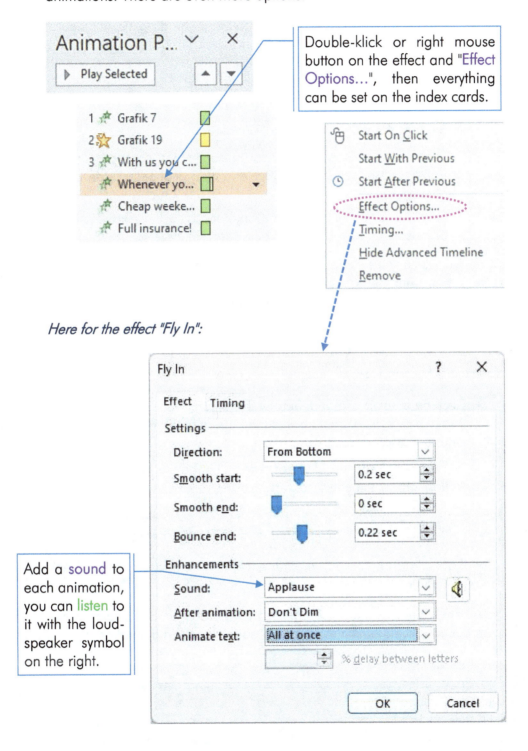

Double-klick or right mouse button on the effect and "Effect Options...", then everything can be set on the index cards.

Here for the effect "Fly In":

Add a sound to each animation, you can listen to it with the loud-speaker symbol on the right.

If the sound examples are not enough for you, you can load a piece of music from your data carrier at the bottom of the drop-down list with "Other Sound...".

These are the two most important ways of setting, above for setting an animation via the animation area, for selecting an animation using the expansion arrow above for animations.

The animations from the "Exciting" category are of course ideal for our sports car rental company, which can be found in the drop-down menu or the "Add animation" icon under "More Entrance Effects...".

➢ Assign appropriate animations to all three text blocks, then start the full preview as a slide show.

➢ Also adjust the animation control optimally.

↪ Either after clicking, if you want to control the process manually with a mouse click, or specify the chronological order as described on page 63.

↪ Now we have assigned some animations to the texts. However, this also works for clip art or other graphic objects.

At our sports car rental company, we can even let the sports car pictures drive with it. With the right sound and the delay set, it looks as if they are accelerating or decelerating, an effective option.

15.2.1 ANIMATIONS FOR OBJECTS

It's actually the same as with text.

➢ Click on a car photo and then try out different effects under Animation or assign an animation with the "Add animation" icon, both ways lead to the same result.

↪ The "Fly In" effect is ideal for a car; change the direction to "from the right" in the effect options.

Now comes the top trick. You can run multiple effects one after the other. Even small film scenes can be created in PowerPoint with this.

➢ If the clip art is clicked, another effect can be added with "Add Animation", e.g., rotate.

Now only the timing has to be adjusted so that the sports car first flies in from the right, then turns after a short break. It works in animation:

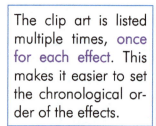

The clip art is listed multiple times, once for each effect. This makes it easier to set the chronological order of the effects.

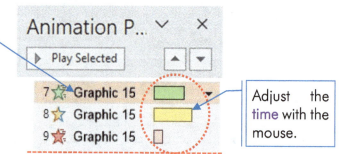

Adjust the time with the mouse.

Here the time is illustrated. Rest your mouse over it, and the set times are displayed. Simply move the lower green bar to the right with the mouse so that this effect starts later.

> ➢ Finally, you can choose an effect, e.g., let the clip art move away with
> fly out or let the car shake with "Swivel" and play an engine sound.

The clipart is now entered several times in the effect menu, so that the speed can be set for each effect.

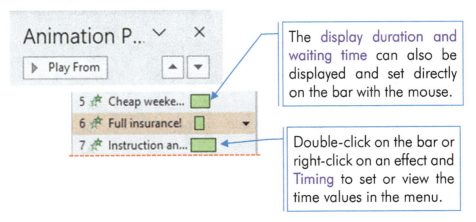

The display duration and waiting time can also be displayed and set directly on the bar with the mouse.

Double-click on the bar or right-click on an effect and Timing to set or view the time values in the menu.

The timing menu:

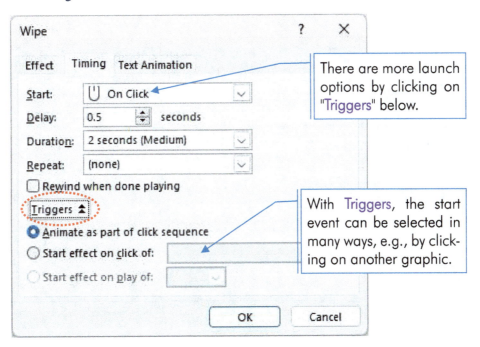

There are more launch options by clicking on "Triggers" below.

With Triggers, the start event can be selected in many ways, e.g., by clicking on another graphic.

Notes: ....

....

....

....

....

....

....

15.3 ANIMATION PREFERENCES

So, we can use "Add Animation" to assign any number of animations to an object or text frame. We can use this, for example, so that as soon as our sports car image is clicked on with the mouse, it shakes and an engine noise sound. This greatly increases the appeal when clients can use the mouse.

➤ Add an effect via "Add Animation", e.g., Pulse. Now you just have to change that this effect only starts when you click on it and not as part of the effect sequence.

➤ Double-click or right mouse button on the new effect in the Animation Pane Area, then select Timing.

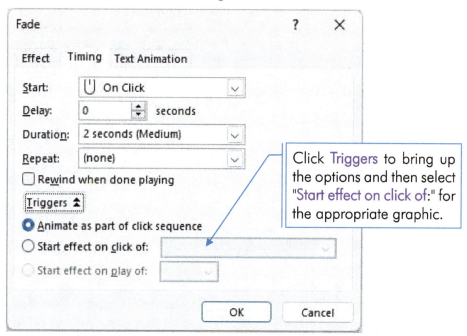

Click Triggers to bring up the options and then select "Start effect on click of:" for the appropriate graphic.

15.4 MOUSE OVER

Unfortunately, we cannot choose in the previous menu that the effect should be executed as soon as the mouse is only moved over the object. But that is also possible, but unfortunately only for sounds and somewhat hidden under Insert/Action:

➤ Click the sports car photo again and select Insert/Action.

◆ What you enter on the "Mouse Click" tab is executed as soon as you click on the element.

◆ With "Mouse Over" it is sufficient to move the mouse over the object.

◆ Neither works in the preview, but can only be tested in a slide show.

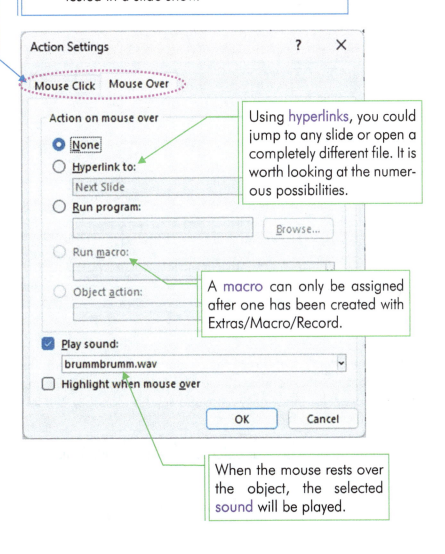

Using hyperlinks, you could jump to any slide or open a completely different file. It is worth looking at the numerous possibilities.

A macro can only be assigned after one has been created with Extras/Macro/Record.

When the mouse rests over the object, the selected sound will be played.

To the macros:

Unfortunately, since version 2013, macros in PowerPoint can no longer simply be recorded, but can only be programmed with Visual Basic, which would be a topic for a separate book.

15.5 DELETE EFFECTS

If you have installed too many effects, you can right-click on the Effects entry in the animation pane on the right and select Remove. Only this assigned effect will be deleted, not the text or image.

15.6 TYPEWRITER AND PARAGRAPH WISE

You can also find the "Typewriter" noise here under Sound. If you fade in a text by word or letter and choose this sound, it looks like it was typed on a typewriter.

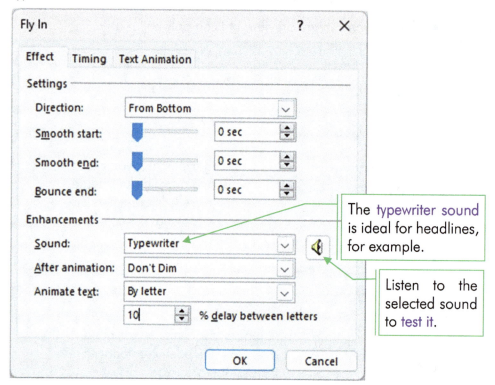

Problem: to increase attention and give the reader time to read, we'd like to fly in each paragraph of text one at a time. There used to be a whizzing or color typewriter effect for this, now we have to set this manually, but this can be done with this special trick:

  ➢ Move the time windows so that paragraph by paragraph is flown in one after the other:

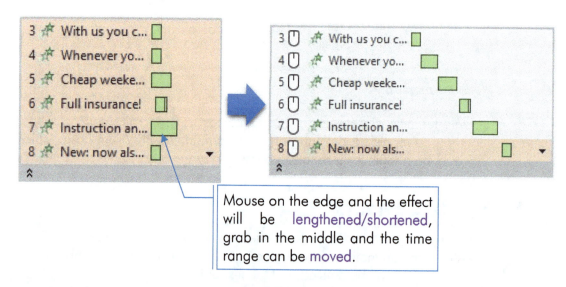

15.7 FILM WITH ADDITIONAL SLIDES

For a change, we can add more slides, on which some cars drive back and forth across the screen with engine noise, before the start slide with the address appears again for a longer time.

[Ctrl]-M

New Slide ⌄

➢ Add a few more slides with [Ctrl]-M and then copy the heading onto them, and delete any existing frames. We could also have used the blank template in Home/New Slide from the drop-down menu.

   ↳ With this you can create movements like in a cartoon by moving a carriage a little further on each slide.

   ↳ If you choose small distances on the first slides and then larger and larger ones, you can simulate an acceleration.

   ↳ Of course, also assign a sound here, which is explained in detail in Chapter 15.6.

Hide the background of the car photo a little:

➢ Insert a car photo, first right-click on it and "Format Picture" to the Effects tab.

➢ For Soft Edges, hide the background a little, then rotate, copy and paste it slightly offset on the following pages.

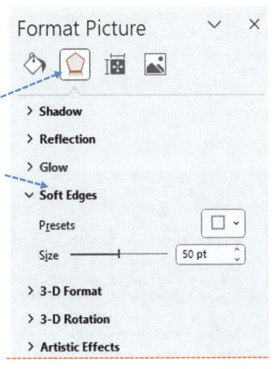

15.8 PREVIEW AND DISTRIBUTE ONLINE

15.8.1 PREVIEW AND CONTROL

Below is the icon to run the presentation on the screen, while you can view and check everything:

More about the views has already been explained on page 28.

15.8.2 DISTRIBUTE ONLINE

The fastest and cheapest way to publish or distribute a presentation, e.g. to customers or members of a work group, is via the Internet..

The following methods are available:

♦ The following manual work is always possible, since MS PowerPoint is no longer required for playback:

   ↳ Export the presentation as a video when recording and send this video by e-mail or play it in an online meeting, e.g., in MS Teams.

   ↳ In the Record menu you will find "Create a Video".

Create Video

♦ Under File/Share/Present Online two ways possible:

   ↳ Save on the MS online storage OneDrive and share from there

   ↳ or export as PDF or presentation and send by email.

First to the second option, send by email:

An email is simply sent in which the presentation is already included as an attachment, either as a presentation or as a PDF file. After an email recipient address has been entered, the email can be sent.

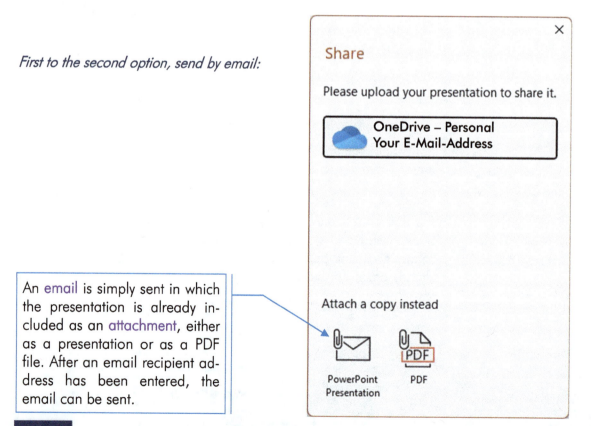

Easier Alternatives:

♦ Using the well-known File/Save As command, you can create a PDF file and also save the presentation to another location for distribution. In both cases, the created file can then be sent as an email attachment using your email program.

     ✎ Particularly if you send mass emails or already have distribution lists, these are easier to select from your standard email program.

     ✎ A PDF file can also be generated using File/Print and the "Microsoft Print to PDF" printer.

Distribute Online:

With the first option, you can upload the presentation to Microsoft's OneDrive online storage and then determine who should share this presentation with.

♦ There are two options to choose from: "Send link" or "Copy link".

     ✎ In both cases, a link to the copy uploaded to OneDrive is created, except that in the first case, the link is emailed via your registered email program, in the second case, the link is only created and copied so that you can then manually forward it by email.

     ✎ In both cases, it is important to select whether the presentation can be edited or only viewed, as well as to select the recipients.

     ✎ The useful function of setting an expiration date for this link is only possible when logging in to Microsoft 365.

Little Exercise:

➢ Create a PDF file of your presentation and send it via your email program to yourself or to friends with a request to return it.

➢ Create a link using the first option "OneDrive..." and send it by email to yourself first so that you always have the link available

     ✎ This link can be inserted into any browser, then the presentation can be viewed or downloaded there.

     ✎ This allows you to check the link first and then forward it to the desired viewers.

     ✎ If you want to e-mail such links frequently, it is best to create a mail merge address database so that you can e-mail this link to all desired recipients automatically.

15.8.3 RUN AUTOMATICALLY

You can print out the presentation or play it on the screen. An interesting variant is to run a presentation automatically on the screen. This allows the presentation to be played back non-stop, for example on a laptop that is in a shop window or is intended to arouse customer interest at a trade fair.

In order for the presentation to run automatically, two settings must be made.

Set Up
Slide Show

> For "Slide Show/Set Up Slide Show" what was described on page 46, e.g., "Browsed at a kiosk (full screen)".

Now for the second required slide transition adjustment.

15.8.4 SLIDE TRANSITION

However, the computer still awaits input in order to continue. In order for this to take place automatically, optimal expiry times must be specified.

On page 62 we already presented the setting options for "Transitions", where the changeover times to the next slide can be specified manually, and in this chapter, e.g., 15.6, the possibility of manually setting the expiry times of the effects on a slide was explained.

Another very helpful option is to let the presentation run and, if a slide transition is desired, to initiate this with a mouse click, the times defined with this can then be saved.

> This can be done with Slide Show/Rehearse Timings:

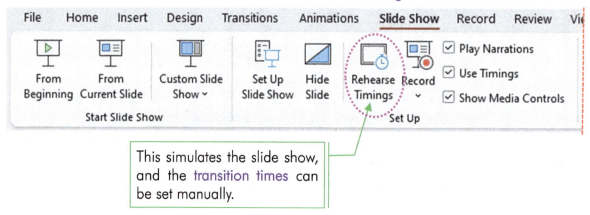

This simulates the slide show, and the transition times can be set manually.

> The control symbols appear at the top left:

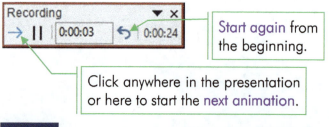

Start again from the beginning.

Click anywhere in the presentation or here to start the next animation.

♦ If all animations of the slide are finished, the next click will switch to the next slide.

♦ When all animations on all slides have been clicked through, you will be asked whether you want to save these clicked times or not.

↳ It is especially important not to save unless you are absolutely sure that you want the new expiry times to be permanent

From Beginning

At the bottom, almost invisible when the slide background is light, these symbols are shown, with which you can scroll both forwards and backwards. These icons are also present when you play a slide show (Slide Show/From Beginning) instead of Test Timing:

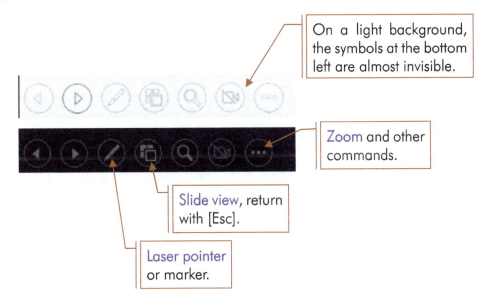

On a light background, the symbols at the bottom left are almost invisible.

Zoom and other commands.

Slide view, return with [Esc].

Laser pointer or marker.

Complete exercise:

➢ You could add any other pages, e.g., with price tables or where individual sports cars are presented or with photos of customers on trips.

➢ Start the above function, set suitable times by clicking, then exit and save.

Notes: ....

....

....

....

....

....

....

16. WITH MUSIC

16.1 OPTIMIZE SOUND

If you run the slide show, you'll notice that most of the effects have no sound. So, we should add music for better impact and attention.

To solve this problem, there are two ways:

- ♦ You are looking for a different finished engine sound.
  - ↳ Soundtracks are included on many CDs/DVDs. If you have a large hard drive, you can collect it in a Music folder and use it when needed. There are also many such sound collections on the Internet, from which many titles can also be downloaded free of charge, search for "wav sounds free" for example. [1]

  - ↳ In PowerPoint you can use Insert/Audio/"Audio on My PC..." to insert music that you load from your hard drive or to record from a piece of music or video that you are currently playing with "Record Audio...", especially suitable for incorporate only short sequences from music videos into the presentation.

- ♦ We can create the engine sound ourselves by modifying a similar sound in an audio program and copying or shortening it to the appropriate length.
  - ↳ Many sound programs can be found free of charge on the Internet, e.g., audacity. Simply search the Internet, for example, for free audio editor or directly for Audacity.

In the previous variants, we first have to find the sound files. Therefore, the next alternative is not to be despised.

- ♦ It is much faster than the often-difficult search for a suitable piece of music if you record it yourself.
  - ↳ Every computer today has a microphone input and with a little musical talent, for example, a hum-hum that does not correspond to the ready-made mush can be recorded. You will find the recording function again in an audio program.
  - ↳ Or record videos on the go with your smartphone or use videos from YouTube and similar platforms. The sound can then be extracted and shortened accordingly in a video program.

---

[1] Respect copyrights!

About the music formats:

♦ We can integrate almost all music formats into PowerPoint, but since computer music is usually saved in wave format like on a music CD, we look for files with the wav file extension.

  ✎ With wave music, which is used on every music CD, the music is saved with a sampling rate of 44.1 kHz. This means that every second it is chopped up into 44,100 digital signals whose volume is stored.

  ✎ During playback, these impulses are filled into even signals, which is why CD players don't just read the data, but are partly responsible for the output quality.

  ✎ Due to the extremely fine fragmentation, however, there is theoretically no loss of quality compared to analog signals. Analog recorded music means that the vibrations are recorded as they are.

♦ Alternatively, the midi file extension can be used for Midi files in which music programmed in the PC is stored, as used by electronic keyboards.

  ✎ Original instruments were recorded and the tones were individually saved digitally.

♦ Music is often also stored in mp3 format, which offers the advantage that the file size of the tracks is very small, because mp3 was developed for portable playback devices in earlier times when data carriers still had very little capacity. Disadvantage: the very deep and very high tones are no longer available, therefore no longer ideal for presentations that are shown in larger rooms with larger speakers.

16.2 SEARCH MUSIC

➢ You will find the search button at the Start or in Windows Explorer, enter *.wav there to search for wav music files. In Windows Explorer you can first choose which drive to search, so this is the more recommended option.

  ✎ On page 72 we have already searched for images using this procedure.

16.3 EDITING IN THE MUSIC PROGRAM

No successful presentation without sound. We will demonstrate how to edit an audio track using the free program Audacity (other programs usually work according to the same scheme).

➢ Find, install and launch Audacity or any other program to edit music on your computer.

➢ Find a sound file or record one yourself, then open the sound file in the audio program for further editing.

➢ Immediately save as a new file with File-Save As, e.g., "original name-editing date", so that we do not change the original.

The music program Audacity:

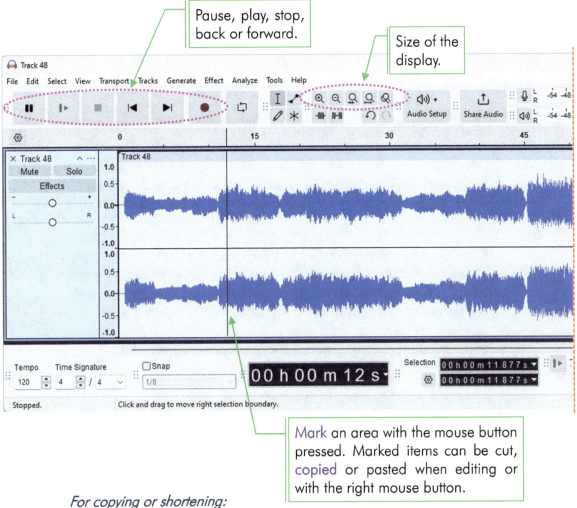

Pause, play, stop, back or forward.

Size of the display.

Mark an area with the mouse button pressed. Marked items can be cut, copied or pasted when editing or with the right mouse button.

For copying or shortening:

➢ Instead of holding down the mouse button, you can use the direction keys to select and deselect areas while holding down the [Shift] key. This is more accurate and relaxed than with the mouse button pressed.

➢ Copy and paste again, etc., until the piece of music is significantly lengthened or e.g., cut out beginning and ending sections to get only a short excerpt.

Additional:

♦ Instead of marking areas, another procedure is often used, the piece is "cut" in two places, then this now detached piece or the areas before and after it can be deleted, copied or moved.

♦ Note the many effects in the corresponding menu item.

Extremely extensive for a free program, easy to use, but of course a bit confusing at first due to the many functions.

➢ If you like the sound and the length is about right, save as a copy and close.

16.4 INSTALL SOUND

You can use the "Insert/Audio/Audio on My PC…" command, but this loads the loaded music file as a separate object in the Animation Pane window.

We want to assign sounds to the car flying in and then driving away. That's why we choose the following method.

➢ In Chapter 15.7 we had created additional slides with an apparently moving sports car, now we will assign the corresponding sound to this sports car.

➢ Click on the sports car on the first slide and in the animation pane on the graphic, the corresponding graphic is marked because we had previously clicked on the graphic with the sports car, with the right mouse button, then select Effect Options.

In the Effect Options menu, you can select a sound on the "Effect" tab:

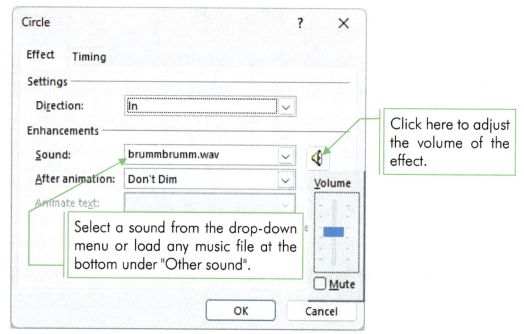

➢ Match the sound to the graphic on each slide that simulates the movement of the sports car.

➢ Then let the presentation run and check the length of the music, if necessary, lengthen or shorten it in the music program and then insert it again in PowerPoint.

> Like good films, good presentations need quality music. Although this is quite labor intensive, it is worth working into sound files and audio programs.

5th Part

TEMPLATES

Create master slides and templates, drawing, WordArt, chart and table

17. TEMPLATE AND MASTER SLIDE

Very often one of the numerous, beautifully designed templates is used in PowerPoint and only the text is entered. Firstly, this is too easy, secondly, the essentials have already been described for this and thirdly, for professional work, a separate design must occasionally be used if, for example, the company logo or company colors are to appear in the background.

That's why we're going to look at the background slide in this exercise and generate our own background slide. A chart is then created and a date inserted. So that we can get to know the functions, let's start from scratch without a template.

> Each page has a background layer that contains the graphic elements: lines, fillings and geometric elements. Using the master slides is not necessary, but has the advantage that you can create slides with the same arrangement and setup (fonts, colors, graphic elements, etc.). This makes a presentation look much more professional. As a simple alternative, this could also be achieved by creating more slides by duplicating them.

What is arranged on the background page is shown on each slide, so that you can place text frames on each page in front of this background, for example. That is why only what should really be visible on each slide should be arranged on the background slide.

Several filled elements, e.g., rectangles, can be superimposed on the background foil in order to obtain different filling settings. Of course, different background slides can also be used within a presentation, e.g., if a completely different background is to appear from a certain slide onwards.

> In PowerPoint there are no styles like in MS Word or styles like in other programs in which text and paragraph settings are saved and can therefore be called up identically at any time, but we can adapt the preset text styles on the master slide as desired and thus as text - and use paragraph presets.

17.1 OVERVIEW SLIDE MASTER

Each presentation has a background slide (Slide Master). On this are the frames for the background. This allows these frames and background to be present on every subsequent page of the presentation, allowing for a consistent design.

We will start a new, empty presentation to create our own design on the master slide.

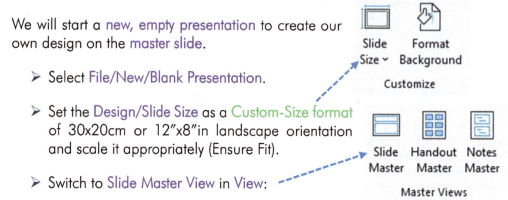

- ➤ Select File/New/Blank Presentation.

- ➤ Set the Design/Slide Size as a Custom-Size format of 30x20cm or 12"x8"in landscape orientation and scale it appropriately (Ensure Fit).

- ➤ Switch to Slide Master View in View:

On the left you will find numerous suggestions for slides:

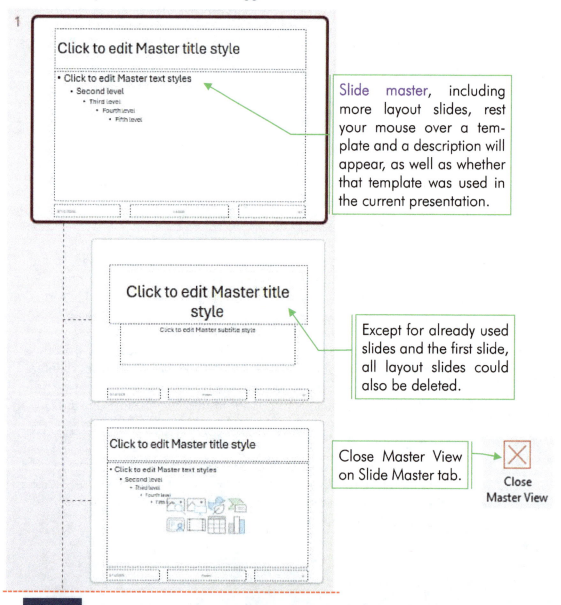

Slide master, including more layout slides, rest your mouse over a template and a description will appear, as well as whether that template was used in the current presentation.

Except for already used slides and the first slide, all layout slides could also be deleted.

Close Master View on Slide Master tab.

17.2 EDIT MASTER SLIDES

You can switch to the underlying master slides at any time with View/Slide Master in order to adjust them, and return to the presentation with View/Normal.

You can find it in the toolbar for the Slide Master:

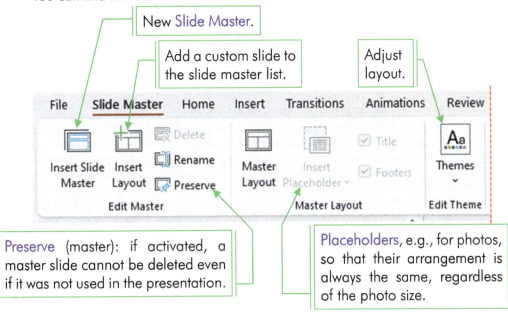

New Slide Master.

Add a custom slide to the slide master list.

Adjust layout.

Preserve (master): if activated, a master slide cannot be deleted even if it was not used in the presentation.

Placeholders, e.g., for photos, so that their arrangement is always the same, regardless of the photo size.

17.3 ADJUST THE SLIDE

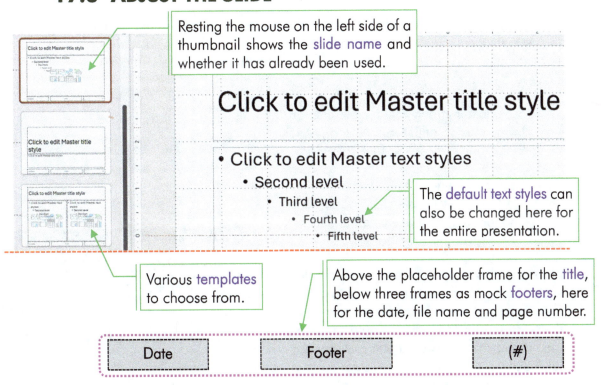

Resting the mouse on the left side of a thumbnail shows the slide name and whether it has already been used.

The default text styles can also be changed here for the entire presentation.

Various templates to choose from.

Above the placeholder frame for the title, below three frames as mock footers, here for the date, file name and page number.

17.3.1 ABOUT THE PLACEHOLDERS

Insert
Placeholder ˅

Note: text boxes inserted with Insert/Text Box could not be changed later on the slides as these are on the master slide so the example text could not be overwritten, this is only for text frames added with "Insert Placeholder" on the slide master view. Select the appropriate placeholder type (text, image, diagram, etc.). Placeholders must not be copied, otherwise the placeholder function will be lost!

♦ A bullet is always automatically inserted in front of the text on new slides in the presentation for both "Content" and "Text" placeholders.

♦ Note on text formatting: sample text with the PowerPoint formatting of the underlying master slide is inserted into new slides in the presentation. Thus, by changing the font formatting of the master slide, we can customize the text preferences.

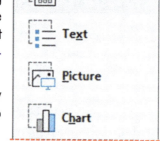

   ✎ Enter your own sample text for each new slide, format it as desired and copy it to the next slides or text frames,

   ✎ create new slides with "Duplicate Layout" together with the font settings or apply the desired formatting with the Format Painter, so text only has to be formatted once.

17.3.2 AS AN EXERCISE: SET UP THE SLIDE MASTER

You can preset the existing text styles on the master slide as desired and thus specify them for every presentation that is based on this master slide. For example, if you create regular reports or something else, you can also achieve a uniform appearance in this way. Let's try this.

➤ Set another strong font for the first font level (master title format), e.g., Arial Black, and choose the font color blue.

➤ Choose different fonts and colors for the text styles (master text format, second level....) so that we can clearly see the effect in this exercise.

Note on deleting master slides: We can delete all template slides, apart from the top master slide, unless "Preserve" has been activated on the Slide master tab, which would of course provide a better overview, but is not very useful, because we could use these format suggestions, but do not have to. Therefore, only delete what you absolutely not want to use, otherwise adjust and arrange the text formats and footers as desired.

17.4 GRID AND GUIDES

We want to create an overhead slide to present business data. To ensure that the text frames and graphics are in the same positions on each page, we can specify the page margins with guide lines.

> ➤ Activate "Snap objects to grid" and set this as described on p. 58: 2 grids per cm = every 0.5 cm.

> ➤ Also set a horizontal and a vertical guide line, here follows the instructions.

Setting new guidelines rationally:

Guide lines from this menu right mouse button/grid and guide lines are quite cumbersome to set. It is easier to do as follows.

> ◆ Hold down the [Ctrl] key and drag away from the original guide lines with the mouse, this creates a copy.

>> ↳ You can move guide lines by holding down the mouse button. The coordinates of the guide line are displayed.

>> ↳ If you drag a guide line out of the presentation, it will be deleted. Or right click/delete on this.

When moving or copying the guide lines, PowerPoint shows the coordinates on the mouse arrow, which simplifies the appropriate arrangement.

17.5 HEADER AND FOOTER

Here you can, for example, add the date, the number of the slide or your name. However, this is only possible if you have not deleted the placeholders for the footers (see figure on page 99.

> ➤ Since headers and footers should appear on every page, they must be created in the slide master view, click on the frame for the footer and enter the desired text.

>> ↳ Although the name is a footer, you can position the placeholder anywhere on the page, i.e., also use it as a header or simply insert additional placeholders.

> ◆ On the slide master tab, you can show or hide a header with "Title" and the same with "Footers".

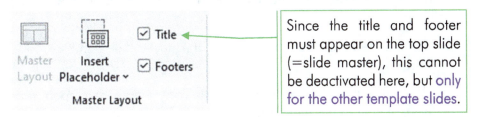

Since the title and footer must appear on the top slide (=slide master), this cannot be deactivated here, but only for the other template slides.

♦ On the Insert tab you can insert both the date and the slide number, e.g., in the header or footer. Note the "Update automatically" option for the date if you always want to display the current date.

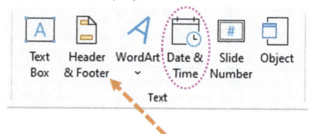

17.5.1 SET UP HEADER AND FOOTER

With the previous symbol you can open the menu for the header and footer, in which you will find interesting setting options:

♦ You can display the date (updated automatically or fixed) and the slide number.

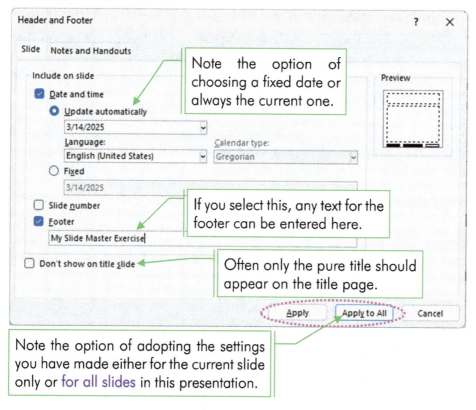

17.5.2 RESTORE HEADER OR FOOTER

If the placeholder boxes are already cleared, you could restore the default as follows:

➢ Start any new presentation, then go to the master slide with View/Slide Master,

➢ Check the three preset footer boxes, copy them, then open your presentation, go to the master slide and paste it there.

17.5.3 AS AN EXERCISE: SET UP A HEADER OR FOOTER

➢ While holding down the [Ctrl] key, drag copies of the guide lines outwards to specify the margins.

➢ Put an updated date in the header and display the slide number.

➢ Display the following text as a footer: © Stroller Fun Ltd.

17.6 SAVING YOUR OWN MASTER SLIDES

➢ Delete some superfluous master slides (right-click on them in the preview area and delete) – the first slide and those already in use cannot be deleted, so it is best to start from the bottom.

➢ Save the template presentation set up in this way as exercise master slides. Important:

    ↳ Select a folder for "Save as" or switch to the detailed menu with "Browse", then switch to PowerPoint Template (*.potx) under File type.

> Note that the PowerPoint Templates folder C:\Users\Username\-Documents\Custom Office Templates was automatically selected. More on this in Chapter 18.6.

    ↳ You have to decide: if you save in this template folder, the template can be selected next to the other templates under File/New, but you must remember to back up these self-created templates when backing up your data.

    ↳ Or you save in your default folder, which you should also save regularly, but then have to switch to this folder to use this template.

➢ Close it, start a new, empty presentation and look under View/Slide Master to see if the original master slides are still there.

    ↳ Everything should still be there as before. So, don't worry, changes to the master slides only apply to our current and future presentations based on this template.

➢ Then close this presentation without saving.

➢ Now start a new presentation based on this slide: File/New, then switch to Custom and under "Custom Office templates" you should find our just created and saved template.

Office   **Custom**

17.6.1 APPLY MASTER SLIDES

We have just created our own somewhat crass master slides in order to learn how to use them. Now it's about creating your own presentation with these template slides, i.e., using the master slides.

♦ So far, we've only preset the fonts and set up the footer.

♦ In the next chapter we will beautify the exercise with graphic elements and fill it with appropriate content.

♦ As this is going to be a monthly report that will be constantly updated with data, we will develop the underlying master slide and the first monthly report in parallel, alternating between the master slide and the presentation, depending on whether we only want the current presentation or the presets for want to edit all future ones.

17.7 COLOR BACKGROUND

Next up is the slide master.

➤ First assign a colorful background to the entire master slide with Slide Master/Background Styles/Format Background..., this time for picture or texture fill.

We introduced the basics of fillings in Chapter 12, now let's try picture or texture fill.

Right mouse button/
Format Background

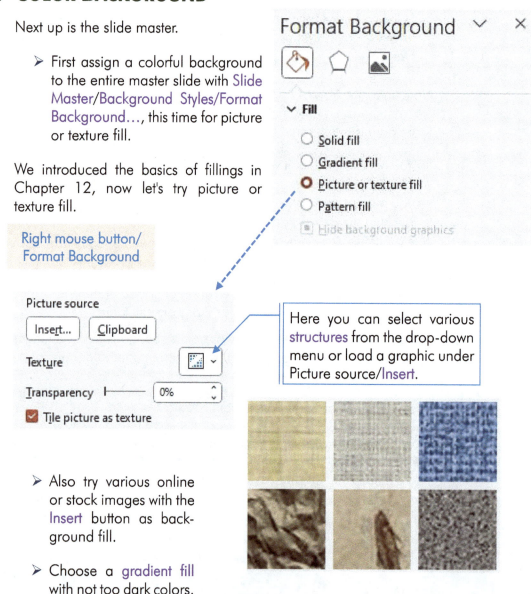

Here you can select various structures from the drop-down menu or load a graphic under Picture source/Insert.

➤ Also try various online or stock images with the Insert button as background fill.

➤ Choose a gradient fill with not too dark colors.

18. DRAWING OBJECTS, TEXT BOXES

Now we will finalize the template and draw for it as well as preset text boxes. Of course, you could use a graphics program to professionally draw a company logo, for example, save it and insert it in PowerPoint with Insert/Pictures/This device.

Then it makes sense to save in the format of the graphics program, but to export the finished drawing in the wmf format, since this format can be inserted into Microsoft programs without any problems. You can find more information about this in our books on CorelDRAW, for example.

18.1 LOAD CLIPART

Just as we load clip art, we could load a photo (Insert/Pictures), put it on the back, or draw a background. But now we use the very comfortable shapes.

➢ Since the following heading should appear on every slide, we put it on the master slide, so open the master slide exercise for this.

➢ Choose a suitable shape, e.g., a banner from the "Stars and Banners" category under Insert/Shapes.

➢ Adjust the banner as wide as the whole page with the mouse. Thanks to the set grid, this is very easy and absolutely precise.

   ✍ If you keep the [Ctrl] key pressed when enlarging or reducing), this is carried out symmetrically on all sides.

➢ Right mouse button, then edit text, enter Stroller SAMple Ltd., center and enlarge the font appropriately.

➢ If necessary, delete existing text frames.

Set the background color see next page.

Set the background color of the graphic object:

♦ There are a few ways to set the background, e.g.:

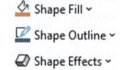

↳ directly at Home under fill effect,

↳ click on graphic, then Shape Format at the top, there you can set the fill under fill effect, the line under shape outline,

↳ right mouse button on the graphic, then format shape, etc.

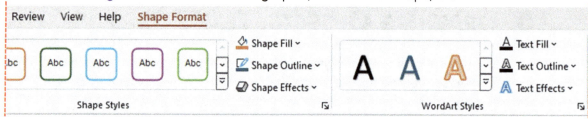

➢ Now select, after you have set the banner color, an arrow, which can also be found under Insert/Shapes, and adapt its width to the slide.

↳ Of course, also set the arrow to the back and set the same fill color with Start/Format Painter for arrow and banner.

↳ Click on the banner, then transfer format and click the arrow.

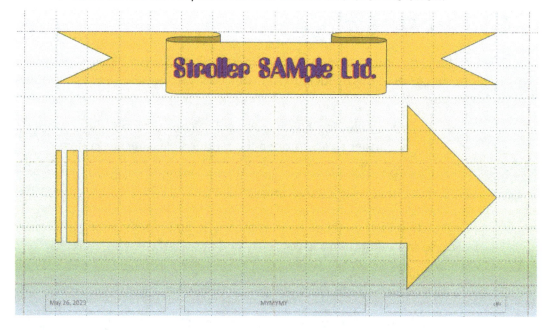

18.2 SELECT MULTIPLE SHAPES

When the background is nicely colored, we can add some graphic elements to emphasize the title and structure of the slide. But before you start drawing, here are a few tips for marking multiple objects, as this makes drawing work a lot easier.

Practical tips for dealing with drawing elements:

♦ You can also move marked drawing elements with the direction keys.

  ✎ Since this is done with a 1mm spacing of the grid, the parts can be very easily and precisely positioned.

♦ You can select several drawing elements while holding down the [Shift] key and adjust or move them together.

  ✎ Grouping is recommended if the elements are no longer to be changed in relation to one another, in order to prevent unintentional moving. If necessary, the grouping could also be canceled again.

♦ If you click on a graphic element, you can use Shape Format/Selection Pane to open a menu in which elements can be listed and marked, or several if you hold down the [Ctrl] key.

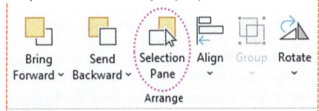

18.3 SUPPLEMENT DRAWING

18.3.1 CIRCLES AND SQUARES

With Insert/Shapes you can insert various drawing elements such as rectangles, ellipses or circles, arrows, stars and much more into the slide. The following applies:

♦ With the [Shift] key pressed, you can

  ✎ Draw circles instead of ellipses, squares instead of rectangles and

  ✎ Draw lines with exactly 0°, 30°, 45°, 60° or 90° degrees.

♦ If you hold down the [Ctrl] key while drawing, the first point is the center point.

  ✎ The [Ctrl] and [Shift] keys can both be pressed, then the first point is the center point and a circle or square is drawn instead of an ellipse or rectangle.

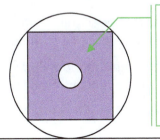

This can also be used to create a copy around the same center point: copy, paste, move the copy onto the original and then reduce the size at the handle while holding down the [Ctrl] and [Shift] keys.

18.3.2 DRAW YOURSELF

Draw a stroller. It is best to
start on a new slide.

The wheels:

➤ A Wheel: Ellipse with Insert/Shapes
while holding down [Shift] = Circle.

↳ If another object is accidentally clicked and moved, undo immediately.

➤ There are many ways to increase the line thickness, e.g., right-click
on the element and Format Shape or directly at Home/Shape Out-
line/Weight.

➤ Then move the wheel with the [Ctrl] key pressed = copy.

↳ It does not matter whether you first press the [Ctrl] key or first grab
and move the wheel and first press the [Ctrl] key on the way,

↳ You can also hold down the [Shift] key, which automatically only
moves horizontally or vertically.

The body as a freehand figure:

Shapes

➤ Now select the freehand
shape for Insert/Shapes
and draw the frame, set a
filling and line color.

➤ On the frame, right
click/Edit Points, you can
reshape the frame if it
doesn't quite fit.

➤ Simply add a line for the
handle.

Recently Used Shapes

Lines

Rectangles

Basic Shapes

Group into a stroller:

So that it becomes a stroller and no longer individual, drawn elements, we
summarize everything.

➤ With the [Shift] or [Ctrl] key pressed, select all drawn elements one
after the other, then select Group under Shape Format.

Group

↳ When marking, note the grab points that appear, which you can
use to determine whether you have marked the desired element.

↳ Note: The symbol is only active if several graphic objects have
been previously selected.

Copy stroller several times:

> ➢ Now the drawn baby carriage is just an element that we can resize, probably you need to resize your stroller, too.

>   ✎ To avoid distortions, keep the [Shift] key pressed.

>   ✎ The line thickness does not change when reducing, it is therefore probably too thick, simply select a thinner line to correct it, this automatically applies to all lines as they are grouped.

>   ✎ Individual elements can still be clicked and changed while holding down the [Ctrl] key, despite being grouped.

> ➢ Then copy the stroller several times while holding down the [Ctrl] key and arrange it appropriately.

It should look something like this:

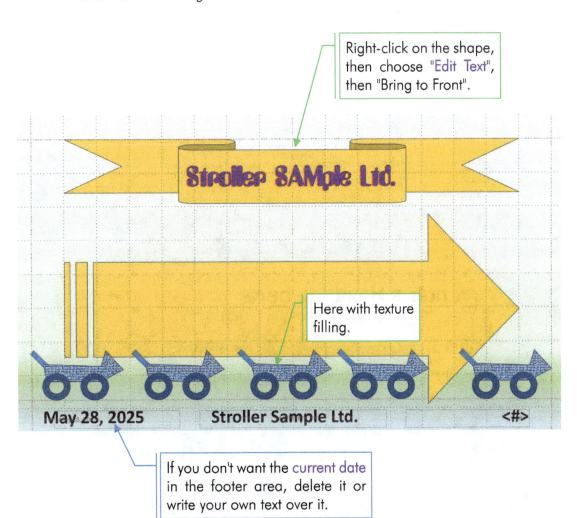

Right-click on the shape, then choose "Edit Text", then "Bring to Front".

Here with texture filling.

If you don't want the current date in the footer area, delete it or write your own text over it.

18.4 PRESET TEXT FRAMES

What good is a background slide without text? We want to create two more text frames or format the existing ones accordingly if you haven't already deleted them.

> The company name Stroller Sample Ltd. should appear on every slide, so we wrote it on the slide master. Now we want to create text frames as placeholders that will later be overwritten by our own texts. The theory for this was discussed in Chap. 17.3.1 already addressed. Since these placeholders should not be identical on every slide, "Insert Placeholder" is disabled on the top master slide.

Insert Placeholder ˅

➢ On the slide master (View/Slide Master) on the Slide master tab with Insert Placeholder insert a text field above the arrow for headings and a text frame on the arrow that takes up almost the entire page width.

    ✎ As soon as you have drawn a text frame with "Insert Placeholder", the default sample texts of all levels are available. We only leave the main heading in the upper frame and all the others in the lower one.

    ✎ Since the background turned out to be very bold, you could set a slightly transparent rather lighter background for the text frames so that the text is easier to read.

The master slide with the text frames:

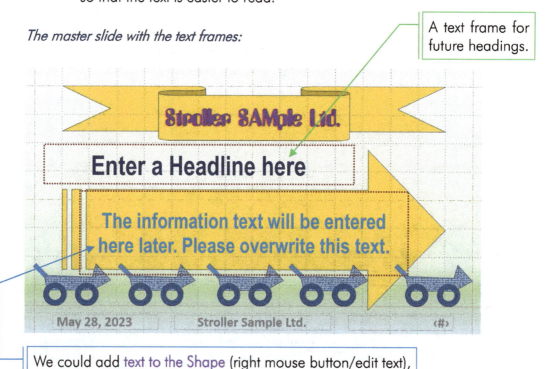

A text frame for future headings.

We could add text to the Shape (right mouse button/edit text), but then the size cannot be adjusted so easily, so it is better to draw a text frame (placeholder), fill it with sample text and preset the text and frame to fit (here centered and blue font).

If these placeholder frames are not needed later, they can simply be deleted.

18.4.1 ADJUST TEXT BOX

A handy option is to automatically resize a frame to fit the text it contains.

♦ Press the right mouse button on the text frame, then select Format Shape and check the option "Resize shape to fit text" on the Text Box tab.

   ↳ In addition to the setting option above, you can also select "Middle Centered" for the vertical alignment, so that the text is also centered in the text frame in the vertical and horizontal alignment.

   ↳ Of course, this has no effect if the size of the frame is automatically set to the height of the text.

♦ You can reach the same menu with right mouse button/Size and Position, only this way shape options/size is selected at the top.

18.5 THE PRINCIPLE OF SLIDE MASTERS

Now it is slowly becoming clear how the slide masters are structured.

At the top of the master title slide, the text styles are predefined and settings that apply to all other master slides, i.e., if, for example, the background fill should apply to all slides, we set them here.

More master slides follow, on which we can predesign different designs (frames, graphics, text styles) and which we can use as templates for our presentation pages, but do not have to use them.

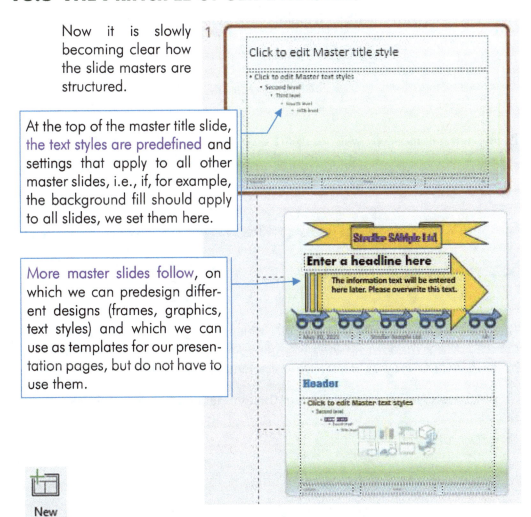

New Slide ⌄

♦ We can later select the defined master or layout slides as a preset in the Normal View with Insert/New Slide.

18.6 SAVE TEMPLATE

Your own master slide is ready, as far as this was useful for understanding the master slides, and could now be used as a template for all company presentations of Stroller Sample Ltd.

There are two ways to save a template:

♦ You can save the template to your folder. However, you then have to switch between this folder and the default folder for templates when selecting the template,

♦ or save to the default folder with the other templates. This is recommended, but you must remember your self-made or customized templates when backing up your data.

To save:

➢ You have probably already saved it – as a normal presentation. In this case, select File/Save As/Browse,

➢ then switch to PowerPoint Template (*.potx) under File type.

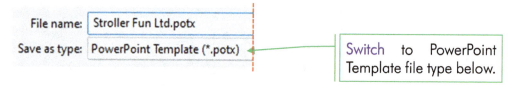

| File name: | Stroller Fun Ltd.potx |
| Save as type: | PowerPoint Template (*.potx) |

Switch to PowerPoint Template file type below.

PowerPoint automatically switches to the default folder for PowerPoint templates, which is displayed at the top of this Save As window.

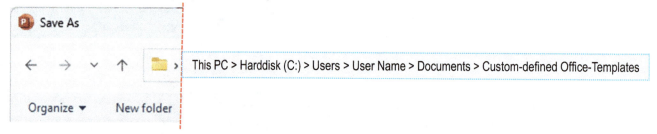

This PC > Harddisk (C:) > Users > User Name > Documents > Custom-defined Office-Templates

The exact folder name in Windows 11, which changes occasionally depending on the Windows version and update, but is automatically selected by PowerPoint as soon as you switch to the Template file type:

♦ **C:\Users\User Name\Documents\Custom-defined Office-Templates**

Complete saving:

➢ Enter the file name and save, then exit PowerPoint.

> Do not forget templates you have created yourself when backing up your data!

18.6.1 USE TEMPLATE

You can select this template like any other template under File/New:

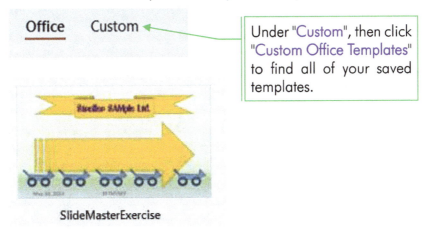

SlideMasterExercise

Under "Custom", then click "Custom Office Templates" to find all of your saved templates.

As already mentioned on page 111, the master or layout slides defined in the template can be selected and used in a presentation in the Normal view with Insert/New Slide as a preset.

This is done in the next section, where we will create the first Stroller Sample Ltd. presentation based on this template.

18.6.2 CUSTOMIZE TEMPLATE

♦ You can adjust the template settings at any time by opening, editing and saving the template file you just saved.

    ↳ When saving the template, specify the PowerPoint template file type again, otherwise it would be saved as a normal presentation.

18.6.3 ALTERNATIVES TO THE TEMPLATES

In the next chapter we can use the template we just created to create our first Stroller presentation.

♦ This way of working with your own template makes sense if presentations that are created in different departments of your company, for example, should have the same design.

♦ An easier way with the same effect would be to resave the first presentation for the new presentations with File/Save As and only change the text.

    ↳ Then there is no need to create your own master slide and the last work is always up to date in terms of design.

19. DIAGRAM AND TABLE

19.1 THE START DIALOG

➢ Restart PowerPoint, then select our newly created design template as the basis for the new presentation as described on the previous page under New/Custom/Custom Office Templates.

↳ In Office you will find all the templates provided by Microsoft.

➢ After "Create" we get a new presentation with the presetting's of the template.

↳ The first slide of the template is displayed automatically, other design slides could be selected with View/New Slide.

➢ Design the first page e.g. as follows:

➢ Then save this presentation in our exercise folder as Stroller_001.

Note the file extensions:

potx for templates, pptx from PowerPoint for presentations. We recommend displaying file extensions, which can be done in Windows 11 as follows:

◆ Open Windows Explorer, click on the three dots at the top and select Options, then on the View tab in the long list, deselect the option "Hide extensions for known file types".

19.2 ADD TEXT AND SLIDES

If you have done everything correctly, you are in normal view and can edit the text frames, otherwise select View/Normal if necessary.

♦ Here we use a simpler method by duplicating the first slide complete with the text frames.

♦ This is ideal if you want all slides to look the same, which is the case in this project, because you want the heading to appear like a header on each page.

➢ Add new slides by clicking on the first slide and selecting "Duplicate Selected Slides" from the drop-down menu under Start/New Slide.

↪ Or right-click on a slide in the preview area on the left, then "Duplicate Slide".

➢ You will receive an identical copy with the text frames, which only need to be overwritten with the current texts.

Click above and a blank slide will be inserted, click below at the arrow area to open the drop-down menu.

➢ Write sample texts similar to those shown.

↪ If necessary, add text frames to the new slides or delete existing ones.

➢ Change the font size appropriately and set a space before and after the paragraphs under right mouse button over the text, then Paragraph.

↪ Check each page immediately in the preview window and, if necessary, move the text frames appropriately in the slide view.

The second page:

For example, "Fly in" the first text again, then fade in the next text with sound.

19.3 A TABLE

Once the text is entered and formatted appropriately, the third page should provide market share data in a table.

➢ Add a third page again: Duplicate Slide.

    ✎ Do not delete the existing texts yet, we can overwrite or delete them at any time.

19.3.1 INSERT TABLE

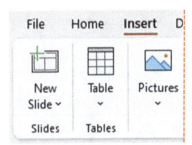

♦ With Insert/Table/Draw Table you could draw or erase table lines with the mouse – rather complicated.

♦ It is more practical to insert a table complete with the desired columns and rows, especially since this specification can be easily adapted, for example by adding more columns or rows.

➢ Click the "Table" icon on the Insert tab when you are on the third page and nothing is selected. This menu opens:

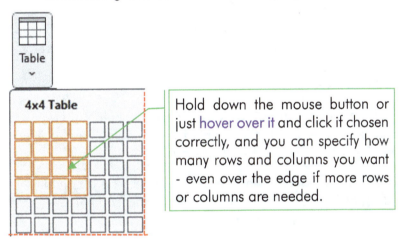

Hold down the mouse button or just hover over it and click if chosen correctly, and you can specify how many rows and columns you want - even over the edge if more rows or columns are needed.

➢ Choose four columns and four rows.

➢ Move the mouse over the edge of the table (top or side) until the mouse pointer changes to a four-pointed arrow, then you can move the entire table while holding down the mouse button.

➢ You can see that we don't need the text frames. Delete the text frame in the arrow and place the table there instead.

    ✎ To delete, click the frame on the line, then [Del].

    ✎ The table can be easily clicked and moved along a line by holding down the mouse button.

19.3.2 FORMAT TABLE

The table is first inserted in a standard size and has to be formatted appropriately, which now follows.

When a table is clicked, the two tabs Table Design and Layout appear at the top of the command categories, where you will find all formatting commands for tables:

- ◆ Table design: graphical settings such as colors, etc.

- ◆ Layout: Set rows and columns ...

- ➤ Choose an appropriate design for the table at Table Styles.

- ➤ Now you can enter some values in the table:

	Stroller	Competitor 1	Competitor 2
2023	123.000 €	55.000 €	99.000 €
2024	177.000 €	66.000 €	101.000 €
2025	255.000 €	46.000 €	95.000 €

You can grab an outer table line with the mouse and thus move the entire table.

When you move the mouse over a column or row line, the mouse arrow changes to a double-headed arrow.
You can then move the column or row line while holding down the mouse button.

Problem last column on the right:

- ◆ However, the previous does not work for the last column. Here you can only set the entire table width at the middle handle, which changes the column width of each column.

- ◆ The same problem occurs when you double-click on a column line to automatically adapt the column width to the content. This also does not work for the last column.

  - ↳ Then use Table Layout/Distribute Columns to automatically adjust the column width.

View   Help   Table Design   **Table Layout**

Distribute Rows

Distribute Columns

Text Direction ⌄

Basic table settings for practice:

- ➤ Arrange the table appropriately and set the entire width appropriately.

- ➤ Automatically adapt the width to the content of the left-hand column with the years by double-clicking on the column line.

- ➤ Then mark the other three columns with the mouse button pressed, either within the table from top left to bottom right or above the table when the mouse cursor changes to a thick arrow, and set their width exactly the same with "Distribute Columns".

19.3.3 THE TOOLBAR

If you click on a table, the main items table design and layout appear at the top of PowerPoint, with the former you will find important frame settings:

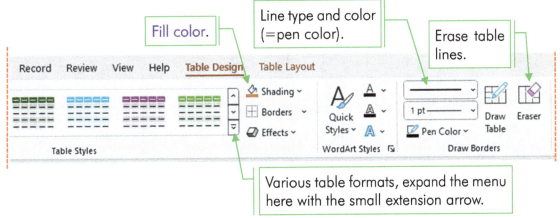

To the frame lines:

♦ [Ctrl]-a marks the entire table if it was clicked. If the table is marked, all lines can be set for frames.

♦ Set line type, line color, etc., then draw lines under "Draw table" (also redraw existing table lines) or specify under frames which lines this should apply to.

The change of line colors:

♦ Line colors and also the line thickness and type can only be selected on the far right next to Draw Borders, then the lines for which this change is to be applied must be traced with "Draw table".

✎ Note: You must draw fairly precisely on existing lines, otherwise a rectangle will be inserted.

✎ When finished, press [Esc] to exit "Draw Table".

Note this specialty of PowerPoint:

♦ In the Table Styles you will find many preset color schemes, please expand the menu with the arrow on the right below and take a look at all of them.

♦ You can set the fill color of marked areas under Shading, but if you have selected "Banded Rows" (or columns) on the far left, which means that every second row is a little lighter, this will be lost.

♦ With Borders, the boundary lines can be selected or deselected, which again only applies to marked areas.

♦ With "Effects" the marked areas can be displayed spatially raised.

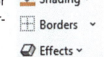

Stroller

19.3.4 THE TABLE COMMANDS

See Table Layout for more table commands.

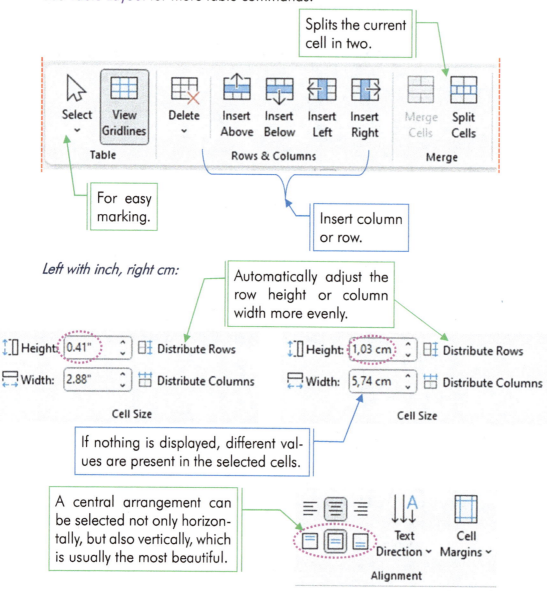

Splits the current cell in two.

For easy marking.

Insert column or row.

Left with inch, right cm:

Automatically adjust the row height or column width more evenly.

If nothing is displayed, different values are present in the selected cells.

A central arrangement can be selected not only horizontally, but also vertically, which is usually the most beautiful.

That's what this slide should be like:

Year	Stroller	Competitor 1	Competitor 2
2023	123.000 €	55.000 €	99.000 €
2022	177.000 €	66.000 €	101.000 €
2021	255.000 €	46.000 €	95.000 €

June 1, 2023   Stroller Sample Ltd.

19.4 CREATE A CHART

We now want to create a chart from the values in our table.

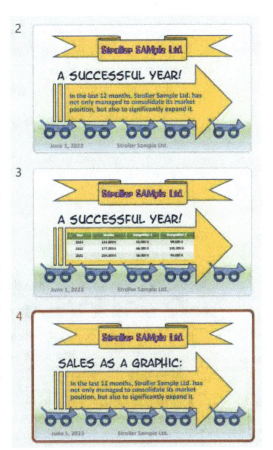

New Slide:

Oops, we need a blank new page again, if you copy the last page with the table, the text boxes would be missing.

➢ Therefore right-click on the page 2 in front of the table, then duplicate the layout and

➢ then simply drag it behind the page with the table in the outline area so that this slide becomes the last page.

➢ Enter "Sales as a Graphic" as the heading and delete the text frame in the arrow.

Values for the chart:

➢ Mark and copy the values of the table (including the headings).

  ✎ If you want to mark from the top left with the mouse button pressed, you usually move the table, then immediately undo. It is easier to mark from the bottom right to the top left.

➢ Then go to the next page after the table and insert a chart on the Insert tab, choosing a template of your liking.

Chart

➢ In the window that appears, similar to MS Excel, first delete the existing example values, then paste the copied ones.

First paste the values without formatting:

In this data table we want the values without formatting, just select "Match destination formatting" on the Smart Tag on the right.

Set column width:

If the columns are too narrow, only "####" will be displayed instead of the values. So, we should rather format the column width a bit too big.

At the top between two column tabs, you can set the column width by holding down the mouse button.

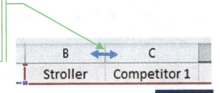

Adjust window size:

The overall size of this data window can also be adjusted, which is highly recommended so that as much data as possible is visible. To do this, move the mouse over the edge of the window, as soon as a double arrow appears, the window size can be set with the mouse button pressed.

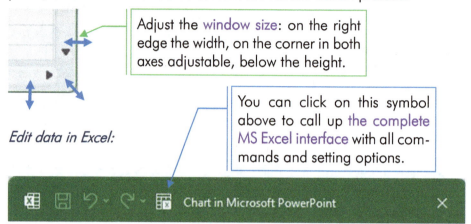

Adjust the window size: on the right edge the width, on the corner in both axes adjustable, below the height.

Edit data in Excel:

You can click on this symbol above to call up the complete MS Excel interface with all commands and setting options.

- ♦ In Excel, you can not only insert formulas for calculations, but also, for example, set the arrangement (centered, etc.) or font formatting (bold, font size, etc.).

- ♦ You can go back again by closing the Excel window with the X symbol at the top right. However, the data table is then gone in PowerPoint. This can be opened again with the right mouse button on the diagram and "Edit data".

- ➢ If there is still one empty line too many selected, grab the selection exactly at the corner point and move it upwards until only data is selected.

The data table set as desired:

Note the useful undo option if something doesn't turn out the way you want.

The window can be moved at the top.

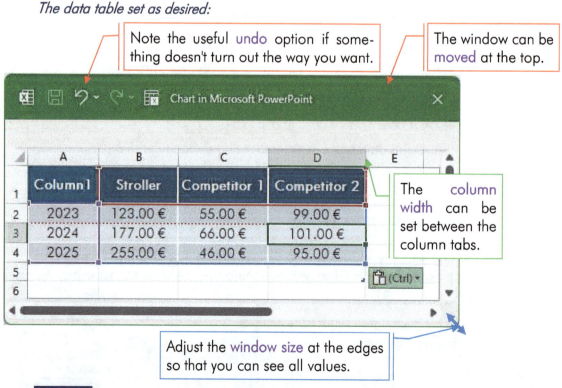

The column width can be set between the column tabs.

Adjust the window size at the edges so that you can see all values.

19.5 EDIT CHART

The diagram can still be visually optimized:

♦ Each element of the diagram can be clicked and then adjusted, e.g. right-click on the diagram and edit data or right-click on the legend and then format legend.

   ✎ When formatting the legend, for example, the position could be changed, e.g. at the top, where there is more space.

   ✎ If you press the right mouse button on the legend, for example, you can turn it off, set its font or arrange it differently.

♦ Right-click on the diagram and change the diagram type, then you can choose a different diagram template, e.g. line representation or bar.

♦ As a further alternative, you could also right-click on the label axis and select font, then select the highly compressed font Arial Narrow, for example.

> This allows you to adjust all sorts of things. You only need to press the right mouse button on the element you want to change.

➢ Now fit the diagram into the arrow at the corners.

When you click on the diagram, these symbols appear on the right:

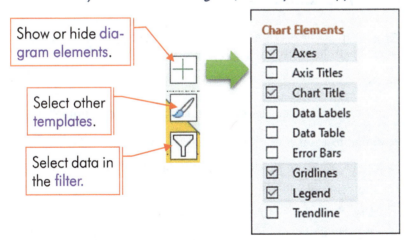

➢ Turn off the chart title, which is already in our heading, and also the data labels.

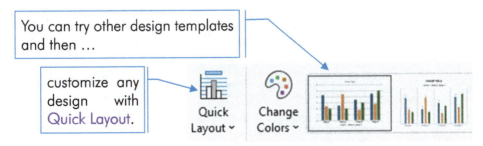

For example, the finished graphic could look like this:

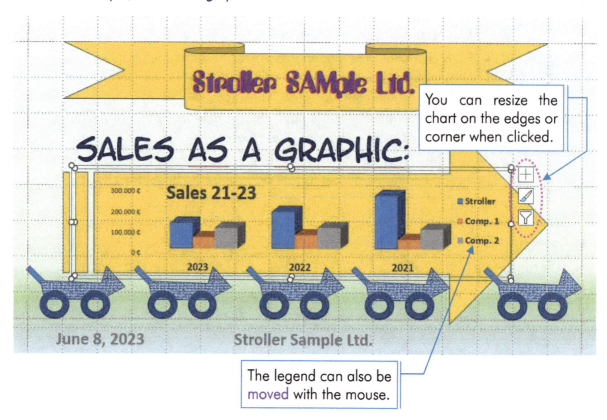

The legend can also be moved with the mouse.

19.6 INSERT OBJECT OR EXCEL SPREADSHEET

Not only from Excel, but also files created in any other program can be inserted into PowerPoint with Insert/Object.

Note the two possibilities:

♦ "Create new", for example to create an Excel table in a slide yourself

♦ or "Create from file" to load a finished calculation or graph.

  ✎ Right-click on this object and edit worksheet (or graphic) to edit it,

  ✎ don't worry, the original will not be changed,

  ✎ with open instead of edit you would, however, open and also change the original file!

Depending on which programs are installed on your PC, other object types are displayed:

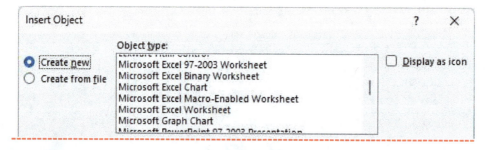

6th. Part

SUPPLEMENTARY

Photo Album, WordArt, Spell Check, Preferences, Export, Overview

20. PHOTO ALBUM

For this last exercise, let's create a template again. Although this would not be absolutely necessary, as there are enough templates, it is also possible without any problems and offers the advantage that you can use it later to create several identical and individually set up pages, e.g., with copyright or a company name.

This time we're going to take the template one step further and we're going to create three template slides: title, regular slides, and special slides for a photo album. Then we can later, when creating the presentation, e.g., insert a normal slide for descriptive texts after some photo slides.

20.1 OVERVIEW OF MASTER SLIDES

➢ Start a new, empty presentation, then first switch to the master slide with View/Slide Master to create the design.

On the left you will find numerous suggestions for slides:

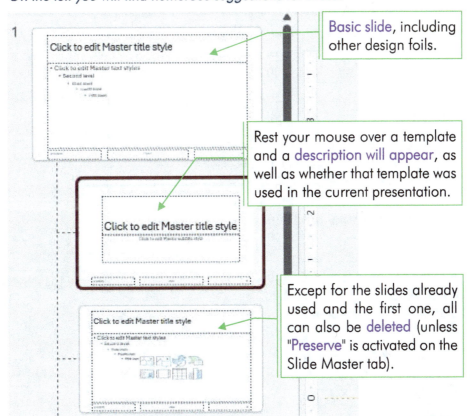

Basic slide, including other design foils.

Rest your mouse over a template and a description will appear, as well as whether that template was used in the current presentation.

Except for the slides already used and the first one, all can also be deleted (unless "Preserve" is activated on the Slide Master tab).

20.2 BACKGROUND ON MASTER SLIDES

Dealing with the master slides is not difficult, but designed somewhat opaquely. Using the master slides is not necessary, but has the advantage that you can create slides with the same arrangement and setup (fonts, colors, graphic elements, etc.). This makes a presentation look much more professional. As a simple alternative, this could also be achieved by creating more slides by duplicating them. In order to fully learn how to use the master slides, we will create three master slides on our own.

➢ Delete the existing master slides as much as possible (right-click on them in the preview area and "Delete Layout").

    ↳ The first two slides "Slide Master" and "Title Slide Layout" as well as those already in use cannot be deleted, so it is best to start from the bottom or

    ↳ click on the third slide, then [Ctrl]-[Shift]-[End] to select all others and delete them at once: right-click on one and "Delete Layout".

➢ Save the presentation as "photo album exercise".

➢ Close it, start a new presentation and look under View/Slide Master to see if the master slides are still there.

    ↳ So don't worry, changes to the master slides only apply to our current presentation.

➢ Then close this presentation without saving and reopen our previously saved exercise.

We now want to create three template types, one for the title slides, one for description texts and one for photos.

This is how it works:

➢ We are still at the View/Slide Master. Color the background of the first sub-slide on the left: right-click/Format Background and, for example, freely set a color gradient:

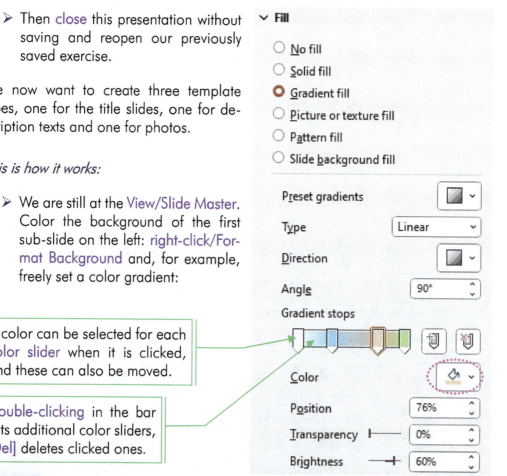

A color can be selected for each color slider when it is clicked, and these can also be moved.

Double-clicking in the bar sets additional color sliders, [Del] deletes clicked ones.

20.3 MASTER SLIDES AND FOLLOWING SLIDES

➢ Then duplicate this slide twice, so we have the same color settings: right mouse button on the left of the preview slide, then Duplicate Layout.

➢ Before you set up the following two slides, under View/Show (expansion arrow) activate Snap objects to grid.

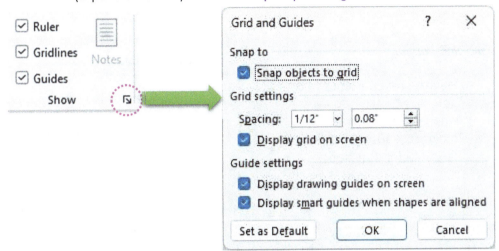

What is on the slide master, the top slide, is necessarily on all other slides, so you can only set up what should actually appear on each subsequent slide

> In our case, since we want to set up different placeholder frames on the following slides, these must not be set up on the first master slide.

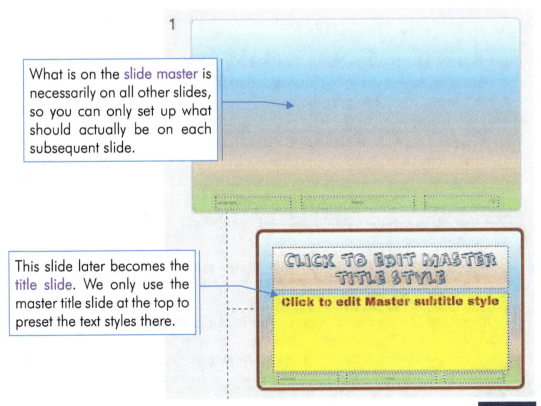

What is on the slide master is necessarily on all other slides, so you can only set up what should actually be on each subsequent slide.

This slide later becomes the title slide. We only use the master title slide at the top to preset the text styles there.

20.4 INSERTING PLACEHOLDERS

Note: text boxes inserted with Insert/Text Box could not be changed later on the slides as these are on the master slide so the example text could not be overwritten or deleted, this is only for text frames added with Slide Master/Insert Placeholder created, select the appropriate placeholder type (text, image, chart, etc.).

On the two slides you just duplicated, adjust all text frames similar to the following image.

➢ Delete existing frames and

➢ when inserting new frames, make sure to use the "Insert Placeholder" function.

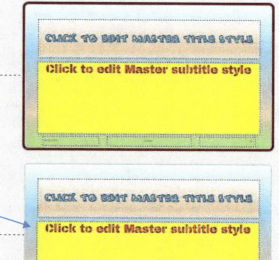

A slide for description text.
In this case, leave only one text style, delete the others, then fill in with sample text.

20.5 ABOUT THE PLACEHOLDERS

◆ A bullet is always automatically inserted in front of the text on new slides in the presentation for both the "Content" and "Text" placeholders.

  ↳ Pre-formatting text according to your wishes can be done using the master text formats on the top slide master.

  ↳ Enter your own sample text for new slides, using a suitable master text level for formatting or formatting this level on the top master title slide accordingly.

  ↳ Later, in new presentations, text can of course be formatted differently than the default if desired.

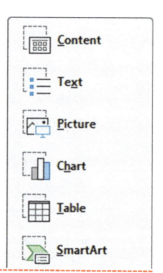

Placeholder frames must not be copied either, as this will result in the placeholder function being lost. If you are faced with the problem that placeholder content cannot be overwritten during a presentation, you probably copied the placeholder in the template.

20.6 A SLIDE FOR PHOTOS

After the slides for introductory text, the slide template for later photo presentations follows.

> ➢ If you haven't already done so, add another slide in the master view.

> ➢ For the photo slide insert two "Picture" placeholders (see previous page), but the displayed text can be changed and formatted as you like.

> ➢ Also underneath are two placeholders "Text", delete the text examples and instead insert and format Description 1 etc.

A first slide for photos:

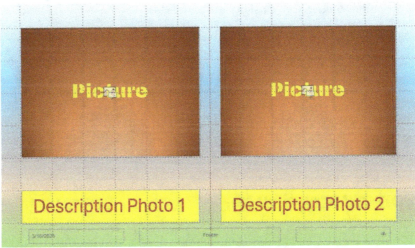

Important, photos can only be inserted into this frame later if you insert a photo placeholder as described on the next page.

This photo-slide is copied into presentations for additional photos, so that all photo slides have the same design.

20.7 PREPARE MASTER SLIDES

We have just created our own somewhat crass master slides in order to learn how to use them. Now it's about creating your own presentation with these template slides, i.e. using the master slides.

> ➢ Before we save the template, we must finally switch to Normal view, otherwise new presentations based on this template would also be opened in the master view.

> ➢ We must also delete the text frames still present in the Normal view so that only our manually set up placeholders appear on new presentations.

20.8 USE MASTER SLIDES

> ➤ Switch to view normal, then save and close the exercise as template, then start a new presentation based on this template.

> ↪ We now only have a blank slide with the background, since we deleted everything on the first master slide to allow for different frames within this presentation.

New
Slide ⌄

> ◆ Now to the next new slide: click on the arrow below Home/New Slide to open the selection menu,

> ↪ here you will find our previously created master slides,

> ➤ and insert a Title Slide and fill it with your own sample text,

> ➤ then delete the existing empty slide with only the background (= the top master slide).

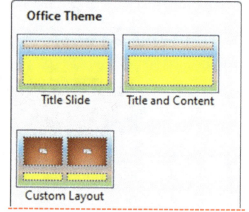

20.9 EDIT MASTER SLIDES

You can switch to the underlying master slides at any time with View/Slide Master in order to adjust them, and return to the presentation with View/Normal.

You can find it in the toolbar for the slide master:

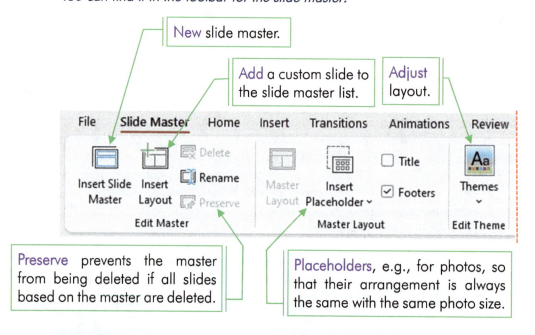

20.10 NEW PRESENTATION

To complete this exercise, we will now create a photo album, using any photos you have on your computer or downloading sample photos from the Internet.

> ➢ Close the master view, i.e., switch to the "Normal" view, create some pages and overwrite them with your sample text, e.g.:

My Photo Album

Your Name

> ➢ Include some photo pages as well, including example photos.

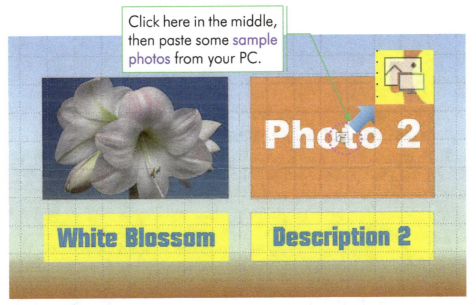

20.11 THE PHOTO ALBUM FUNCTION

Fotoalbum

We have already loaded individual images with this Insert/Pictures/... command, now we will look at the photo album function, which is also located under Insert.

This allows you to create your own slide shows in PowerPoint. Of course, texts, animations or music can also be added to the photos as before.

The difference to manually inserted photos as in the previous exercise is:

♦ The photo album function always starts a new presentation with a title slide and any number of photo slides.

♦ You can select multiple photos at once, each photo will be placed on its own slide so the presentation can be played like a slide show.

Create photo album:

> ➢ Select Insert/Photo Album.

> ✍ Whether you click Photo Album in a presentation or choose New Album from the arrow at the bottom, a new presentation always starts.

Insert   Design   Transitions

Pictures   Screenshot   Photo Album ∨

Images

This means that no photo album can be built into an existing presentation.

The desired photos can be selected in the menu that appears.

Photo Album

Album Content

Insert picture from:

File/Disk...

Insert text:

New Text Box

Picture Options:

☐ Captions below ALL pictures

☐ ALL pictures black and white

> ➢ Find photos you want to include in the photo album, and create some slides of this photo album to complete the exercise.

> ✍ If you cannot find a folder with usable sample photos, search for photos on your computer as described on page 72.

The photo selection menu:

Use this function to select the photos. With the [Shift] key pressed, several can be selected at the same time.

All previously selected photos will be inserted, marking is only possible in order to edit a photo using the symbols: rotate, contrast, brightness. This is only active if ONLY one photo has been marked!

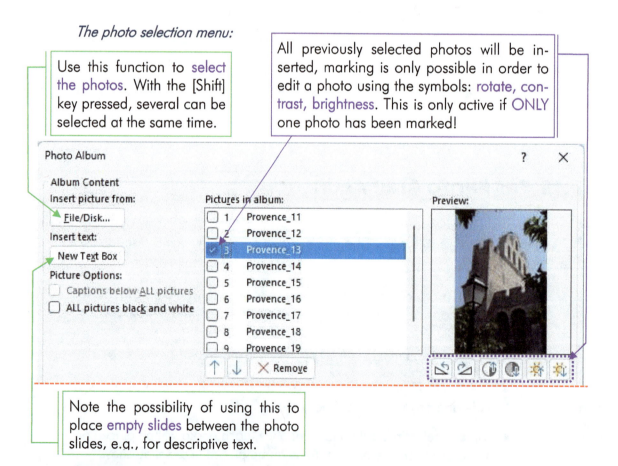

Note the possibility of using this to place empty slides between the photo slides, e.g., for descriptive text.

Create photo album:

> ➢ After "Create" the presentation is prepared.

> ➢ Temporarily set the Slide Show/Rehearse Timings, then run the presentation as a test ([F5]).

Advance Slide

☑ On Mouse Click

☑ After: 00:30.00 ↕

♦ You can also set the display duration for an automatic slide change under Transitions/Advance Slide, but this must be done for each slide.

20.12 OPTIMIZE PHOTOS

If an image is a little too dark or too light, this can be corrected in Power Point.

> ➢ As soon as you click on an inserted photo or clip art, you can switch to the graphic symbols using the "Picture Format" tab.

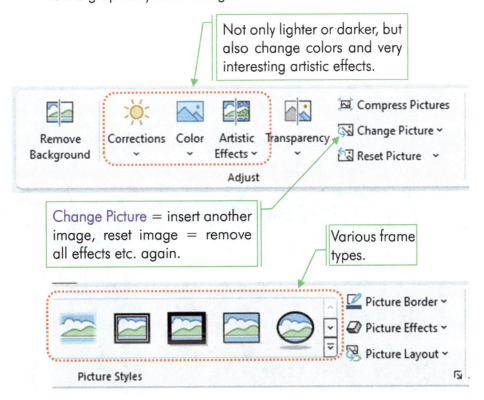

Not only lighter or darker, but also change colors and very interesting artistic effects.

Change Picture = insert another image, reset image = remove all effects etc. again.

Various frame types.

♦ Alternative: press the right mouse button on the photo and select Format (Shape, Graphic etc.), a menu in which e.g., the fill color, shadow, size, brightness etc. can be set.

Other interesting options:

- ♦ Especially if you are using high-resolution images, you can compress them for a pure slide show in order to reduce the file size and thus also avoid stuttering during playback: see figure above:" Compress Pictures".

- ♦ On the far right you will find the "Crop" function, which can be used to cut away the edges of the image. Not only can the format be adjusted, but an image can be reduced to an form as by Insert/Forms, e.g. an ellipse or arrow.

Crop

- ♦ With color you can change the color tone or hide a color with "Set Transparent Color", good to use with semi-monochrome backgrounds to hide them.

Color

  - ♫ Transparency can be set for the entire photo under Transparency, but if the picture has been inserted into a frame, this frame fill color will be visible, not the background. The easiest way is to delete the picture and insert it again without a frame.

Transparency

- ♦ The "Remove Background" function goes one step further, with this you can hide everything except for the desired object, e.g., a dolphin or the blossom.

Remove Background

  - ♫ Use "+" or "-" while holding down the mouse button to mark or unmark areas until the desired one is selected.

Mark Areas to Keep   Mark Areas to Remove   Discard All Changes   Keep Changes

Refine   Close

Sample Page of the Photo Album Exercise:

21. WORDART

WordArt is an additional program with which special effects like in a graphics program are possible: text with shadows, hatching or with spatial perspective, of course in color!

Since you can make an impression with such graphically prepared texts, e.g., for a company logo, especially in a screen presentation, a brief description follows.

21.1 START WORDART

➤ Start a new file with a nice template. You can find the WordArt icon on the Insert tab:

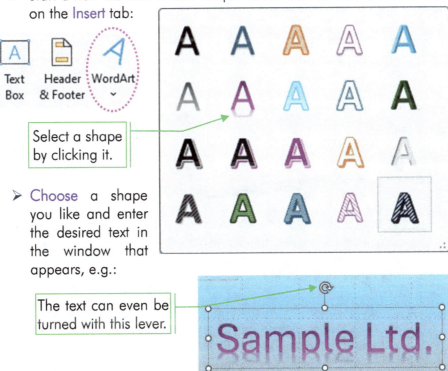

Select a shape by clicking it.

➤ Choose a shape you like and enter the desired text in the window that appears, e.g.:

The text can even be turned with this lever.

Complete! The result with adjusted colors (transparent), a shape effect (Bevel) and rotated slightly:

21.2 SET WORDART

Each pre-selection can be set individually.

♦ Like any graphic, you can move this object with the mouse or change the size at the handles.

♦ As soon as you click on the object, it can be edited again. The drawing tools in Formformat are particularly interesting:

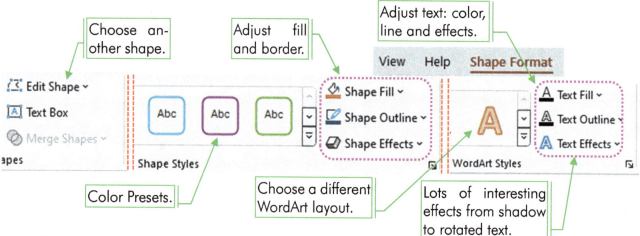

21.3 COLORS AND SHADES

➢ Note that you can also use the small expansion arrow to open full menus for form format:

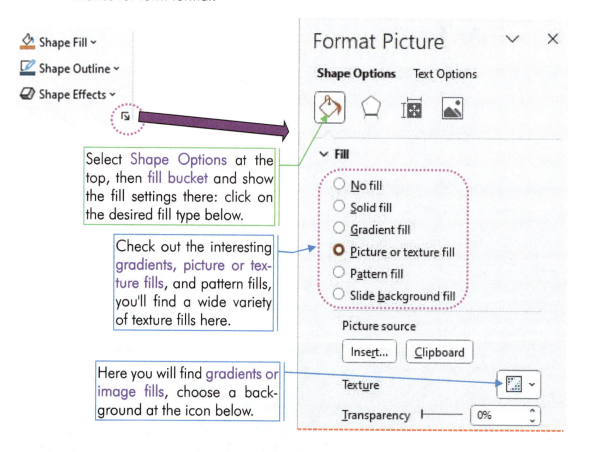

Select Shape Options at the top, then fill bucket and show the fill settings there: click on the desired fill type below.

Check out the interesting gradients, picture or texture fills, and pattern fills, you'll find a wide variety of texture fills here.

Here you will find gradients or image fills, choose a background at the icon below.

For "Shape Styles", select a predefined color fill or set it manually under "Shape Fill":

A round shape was selected for "Edit Shape", color and line thickness were set for this, then a transformation was used for text effects:

With wood filling and spatial elevation for the 3D effects:

➤ Additional effects can be applied to the background for each fill effect, e.g., a glowing border or shadow.

♦ In the case of picture or texture fill, any image could also be used as the background.

21.4 EXERCISE WORDART

Now create an ad with your knowledge:

The text shape can be changed in Text Effects/Transform.

The easiest way to stretch (expanded) text by 5 pt is as follows: mark, right-click, Font, go to the Character Spacing tab.

LETTERS
against money
Paperwork of all kinds takes over:
Writing Office Adler
366-368 N Main St,
Freeport, NY 11520, USA,
Phone (01234) 45 34455

21.5 FLIP AND ROTATE WORDART

Graphics? – Super easy with WordArt. Ideal for PowerPoint slides.

➤ Write and format the following practice example using WordArt:

Set the color gradient:

> ➤ Here, a self-designed color gradient was used for the background by double-clicking on additional color points, for which a color was then selected.

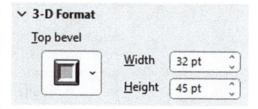

> ➤ Text got a downward flip and light blue glow in Text Options, all adjustable by highlighting the text, right clicking/formatting it and going to Text Options.

> ➤ Finally, a 3D effect was assigned to the shape, a rounded rectangle (Insert/Shapes), which was set to the back (right mouse button/Send to back), in which the height and width were greatly increased.

With Text Effects/Transform, texts can be rotated:

A Text Fill ˅
A Text Outline ˅
A Text Effects ˅

Try some perspectives that others occasionally explore for themselves. You can even arrange text in circles with WordArt!

> ➤ Write as WordArt Carousel-, Operation and A. Funnier with a new line at the end,

> ➤ choose the above circular arrangement, background with texture filling.

An ellipse was deposited, assigned a 3D effect and increased and widened.

The color mix was created by a shadow that was adjusted appropriately.

Because WordArt demands a lot from the computer, you should only use it for a few words and never for longer texts.

Chapter 22

22. DISCLOSURE, HYPERLINKS ETC.

If you publish the file on your computer, e.g., your laptop, there is no problem since you have PowerPoint installed. Then you only need to run the presentation in PowerPoint.

However, it is also possible to play the presentation on another PC without PowerPoint or even publish it on the Internet. Here are a few brief tips.

22.1 SHARE PRESENTATION

With the following command you can save the finished presentation in such a way that it can also be run on a computer without PowerPoint. The presentation can then be burned onto a USB stick, for example, and taken to customers or to a conference.

♦ USB sticks are much more practical than CDs/DVDs for data transport, as not every computer today has a DVD drive because there is no burning process and they are not scratch-sensitive like DVDs.

♦ As an alternative, there would be the option of saving to an online storage device that has been released for a conference group, for example. To be on the safe side, save it on a USB stick or on your own laptop you took with you to the conference.

In File/Export you will find some options for this:

♦ Create PDF/XPS Document: PDFs are particularly useful so that the presentation cannot (slightly) be changed and also looks unchanged on a wide variety of playback media.

♦ Create a Video: here the presentation can be exported to a standard mp4 video file, which enables problem-free playback e.g., on smart TVs or publication on video platforms such as YouTube etc. Since PowerPoint 2021 it is now possible to save the video in 4K quality.

♦ Create an Animated GIF: the gif format is a photo format like jpg, except that several image contents can be shown one after the other. The worst option with partially cut off text, transition times cannot be set - be sure to test before publishing

♦ ... for CD (DVD): as previously mentioned, no longer the best option.

- ◆ Create Handouts: the slides are exported as a table in an MS Word text document.

  - ✎ If the slides are not visible, select everything ([Ctrl]-a) and change the line spacing from exact to single in Start/Format/Paragraph.

- ◆ Change file type: Here the presentation can be exported to a Power-Point slide show, for example, which can be started from Windows Explorer with a double click and then runs like a film without the viewer being able to change anything.

  - ✎ Other target formats are jpg or png photos (each slide is exported to a photo or convert a presentation to a template.

- ◆ Also in the "File" menu, by File/Share, you can save a presentation on the Internet when you share it, as already shown on page 86.

22.2 WATERMARK

Especially before passing on or even publication, the consideration arises of at least protecting a presentation against unauthorized passing on by means of a watermark.

There is no automatic function for this in PowerPoint, so only the following manual procedure would be possible:

- ◆ In an image editing program, e.g., Corel Photo-Paint, manually add a watermark to a photo, e.g., write "copyright: your name" as text and then use an effect to make it not immediately recognizable,

  - ✎ e.g., lighten or, as described in our book on Corel Photo-Paint, convert the text into a mask and then make this masked (=marked) area lighter.

- ◆ Then integrate this photo into the background of the master slide or use it as a background so that it appears on every slide.

22.3 HYPERLINKS

- ◆ Hyperlinks, e.g., to open a web page, can simply be written into any text of a PowerPoint presentation, they would be recognize automatically, or copied there, or you can use the Insert/Link function for this.

  - ✎ This button is only active if a text field has been clicked.

  - ✎ With Insert/Link, the settings menu for hyperlinks is opened, which you can also call up for each hyperlink by right-clicking on a hyperlink and "Edit Link".

  - ✎ In the settings menu, you can also use a link to jump to another slide in this presentation by specifying a slide in "Place in This Document" on the left.

> ➤ Mark a text, e.g., a description page in out photo album presentation, to which the hyperlink is to be assigned, then select Insert/Link.

This menu appears:

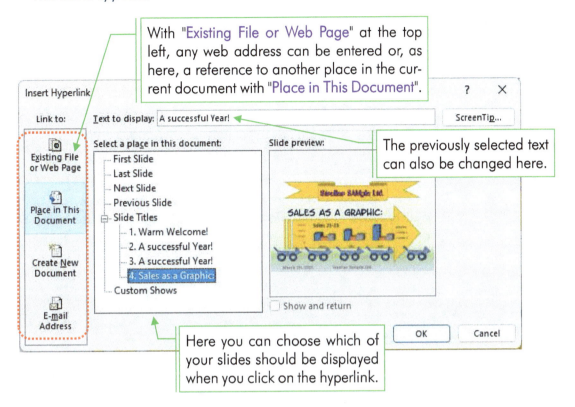

With "Existing File or Web Page" at the top left, any web address can be entered or, as here, a reference to another place in the current document with "Place in This Document".

The previously selected text can also be changed here.

Here you can choose which of your slides should be displayed when you click on the hyperlink.

22.4 COMMENTS

Comment

Comments

♦ Comments can be added with the right mouse button or in the Insert menu.

↳ Comments are not displayed during the presentation and can therefore only be used as explanations or reminders when editing the presentation.

♦ In the Review menu, you can display a comments area so that all existing comments are displayed in a separate window on the right.

↳ Here you will also find additional comment functions:

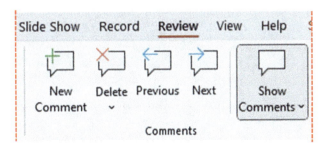

22.5 SLIDES FROM OUTLINE

Slides from Outline…: found on the Insert tab in the drop-down menu under New Slide at the very bottom - a misleading name.

- ♦ You can use this to insert any text document into PowerPoint, which of course becomes a new slide there.
  - ↳ More precisely: PowerPoint chooses a separate slide for each paragraph, if the text consists of numerous paragraphs, you will get just as many slides.

- ♦ It usually makes more sense to open the document (=outline) in the original program, mark what is to be adopted, copy it and paste it into the PowerPoint presentation.
  - ↳ This way is generally more advisable, as you can choose exactly what is to be inserted into the PowerPoint slide, because in the rarest of cases a document should be inserted completely with a separate slide for each paragraph.

22.6 COMPARE AND MACRO

Compare

- ♦ Compare (by Review): if you have sent a presentation, for example by email, and have received it back corrected, you can accept the changes here.
  - ↳ To be on the safe side, first save a backup copy of your original version, e.g., with the date appended to the file name.

Makros

Makros

- ♦ Macro (by View): you can program recurring command sequences as macros and run them later. Rarely needed in PowerPoint.
  - ↳ Unfortunately, it is no longer possible to simply record macros; they have to be programmed in the Microsoft programming language Visual Basic, which would require a separate book.
  - ↳ You can open the Macro function in View.

Notes: ....

....

....

....

....

....

....

22.7 RECORDING

In the Record menu item, you can create videos or audios from the screen, not just from the current PowerPoint presentation, or export the presentation as a video.

It means:

♦ Cameo: this allows you to add a window to the presentation in which content sent from your video camera is displayed live.

♦ "From Beginning" and "From Current Slide" exported as a video file.

♦ Screen Recording: a rectangular area on your screen, not only within the PowerPoint presentation, can be specified to be recorded as a video.

   ♘ Note the inconspicuous, hard-to-see icons that appear in the top center to pull the selection frame, start or stop recording (close this toolbar).

Specify or change the area of the screen to be recorded by holding down the mouse button.

Recording or exit this menu and return to normal PowerPoint.

Start and then stop the re-cording.

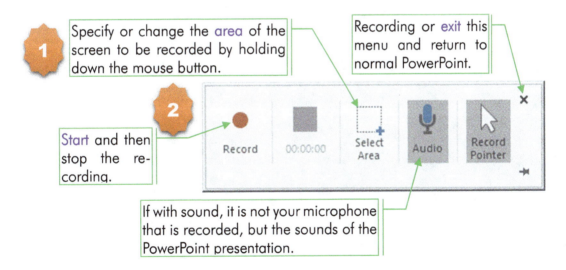

If with sound, it is not your microphone that is recorded, but the sounds of the PowerPoint presentation.

♦ Audio: as the name suggests, only record the audio of the presentation.

♦ Save as slide show: a file with the extension ppsx is generated, which can also be started without PowerPoint, but only on MS Windows computers.

♦ Export to video: the presentation is saved as a video in mp4 format, this video can then be shown on other computers, playback devices, not just with Windows, or on the web.

23. APPENDIX

At the end there is some useful advice for using PowerPoint and other commands and options that are used less often.

23.1 THE SPELL CHECKER

Spelling

F7

- ◆ You can start the spell check in the Review menu with Spelling or with [F7].

You have probably already noticed some red underlined words. This is the automatic spell checker.

- ◆ PowerPoint also uses the dictionary provided with Office.
    - ↳ It compares these words in the dictionary with your text.
    - ↳ If you use a word that is not in the dictionary, it will be marked.
    - ↳ Therefore, the underlined words are not necessarily wrong!

- ◆ With this you can also see the limits:
    - ↳ Especially in the case of technical texts, PowerPoint does not know many words.
    - ↳ You can add the unknown words to a so-called user dictionary.
    - ↳ Useful for recurring technical terms, of course also for your name, street, etc.

- ◆ All Office programs use the same custom dictionary called RoamingCustom.dic (dic for dictionary). Depending on the Office version, this file can also be named RoamingUser.dic or previous without roaming.
    - ↳ All words included in the user dictionary in Word, for example, also apply in PowerPoint and vice versa.

> You can also use the spell checker for different languages, highlight sections of text and select the appropriate language under Review/Language.

Deleting words from the user dictionary:

♦ If you have inadvertently recorded incorrectly spelled words, you can use Windows Explorer to search hard drive C: for *.dic, using the "All subfolders" search option.

   ↳ if several are found, sort by date,

   ↳ open the most recent one with Notepad or Word and simply delete the wrong word, don't forget to save.

23.1.1 THE AUTOMATIC DETECTION

♦ Unfamiliar words are underlined in red as you type.

   ↳ Instead of running the spell checker in a marathon over a long text, it can be corrected immediately.

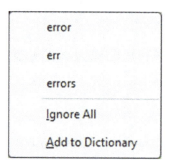

Start correction:

♦ Press the right mouse button on a red un-derlined word, Correction suggestions are now displayed.

You have following options:

♦ If the correct word is there, select the suggested correction.

♦ If your word is spelled correctly but underlined in red, PowerPoint does not recognize this word.

   ↳ Press Add... to add the word to the user dictionary

   ↳ or Ignore All if the word only occurs in this presentation. It will then no longer be circled in red in this presentation, i.e., ignored by the spell checker.

♦ Of course, if you spot the mistake immediately, words can also be changed manually.

23.2 THE PREFERENCES

As with any Office program, PowerPoint can be set under File/Options.

♦ E.g., for document checking you could switch off the automatic spell checking just described,

   ↳ what many PowerPoint professionals do, since we have little but extraordinarily important text with many technical terms, so that this check is often more annoying than useful.

♦ With Customize Ribbon you can, for example, add or delete symbols, set the default storage location with Save, etc.

   ↳ With Save you can also change the folder suggested by PowerPoint for personal templates.

   ↳ The Office design can be selected under General. We recommend to try some designs.

↳ By the way: Right-clicking on the ribbon and "Customize the Ribbon" is a quicker way to get to the settings menu instead over normally File/Options.

♦ A function that is important for professional use can also be found under Save: "Embed fonts in the file".

↳ If this is activated, you avoid the problem that years later the exact font used could no longer be installed on your computer, so that the whole design would be jumbled up.

↳ The file is also displayed perfect on other computers when it is passed on and if you activate "Embed all characters", it can also be edited and changed.

23.3 FILE/INFO

Not only information about the file can be entered here (click on "Properties", then "Advanced Properties"), e.g., title, subject and author, but many properties of the presentation are also displayed, e.g., the file size, how many words are used, the storage location, the fonts used, etc.

♦ In the File menu click on "Properties", then "Show All Properties".

♦ You can also protect your presentation here by Info, e.g., that it can only be edited with a password:

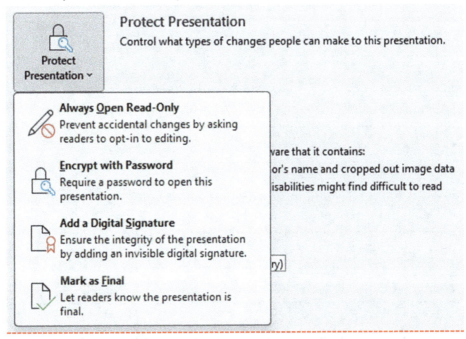

♦ And you can have your presentation checked again automatically here.

Standard shortcuts and keys:

[Ctrl]–s	Save	[Ctrl]–x	Cut
[Ctrl]–p	Print	[Ctrl]–c	Copy
[Ctrl]–z	Undo	[Ctrl]–v	Paste
[Ctrl]–a	Mark all	[Ctrl]–d	Duplicate slide
		[Ctrl]–m	New slide
[Ctrl]–f	Find	[Ctrl]–h	Replace
F5	Start Presentation		
F1 or Help	Help	[Esc]	Break away

[Alt Gr]	^{2} ^{3} { } [ ] \ | @
[Return]	New Paragraph.
[Shift]-[Return]	New line in same paragraph
[Return] at the end of the text in normal view	Start new slide

Notes: ....

....

....

....

....

....

....

....

....

....

....

....

....

....

LINDEMANN GROUP © MSC. (UAS) PETER SCHIESSL

Chapter
24

24. INDEX

LINDEMANN GROUP © MSC. (UAS) PETER SCHIESSL